This book is dedicated to
Nohad Haj Salih's
contagious enthusiasm.
May these ideas bring
peace to his home on the
other side of the sea.

CITIES

PRESS
URE .

CITIES UNDER PRESSURE: A DESIGN STRATEGY FOR URBAN RECONSTRUCTION

Benno Albrecht, Jacopo Galli

•

Research by

Urbicide Task Force

•

Principal investigator

Benno Albrecht

•

Coordinator

Jacopo Galli

•

Researchers

Andrea Fantin, Marco Marino, Serena Pappalardo, Giulia Piacenti, Sabrina Righi, Chiara Semenzin, Elisa Vendemini

•

Young researchers

Alessia Cane, Ambra Tieghi

•

Book design

Stefano Mandato
with Silvia Casavola

•

Editor

Maddalena d'Alfonso

•

Text editing

Dawn Michelle d'Atri

•

Project management

Cristina Steingräber,
Sonja Bröderdörp

•

Published by

ArchiTangle GmbH
Meierottostrasse 1
10719 Berlin, Germany
www.architangle.com
ISBN 978-3-96680-023-5

•

Reproductions

Eberl & Koesel Studio, Altusried-Krugzell, Germany

•

Printing and binding

Memminger MedienCentrum Druckerei und Verlags-AG, Memmingen
Printed on VIVUS89 – FSC®, EU Ecolabel, CO2-neutral paper

•

•

Collaborators of Urbicide Task Force

Emilio Antoniol, Sara Altamore, Wesam Asali, Maddalena d'Alfonso, Alessandro Dal Corso, Alessandro De Miranda, Mauro Frate, Letizia Goretti, Enrico Guastaroba, Anna Magrin, Luca Panzeri, Nicola Pavan, Francesco Rossi, Tania Sarria, Rossella Villani

•

Supporters of Urbicide Task Force

Helena Barrocco, Monica Centanni, Salma Samar Damluji, Abdallah Dardari, Raida Deeb, Farrokh Derakhshani, Alberto Ferlenga, Manar Hammad, Jorge Lobos, Carlo Magnani, Olena Motuzenko, Francesco Musco, Ciro Pirondi, Nasser Rabbat

•

Thanks to

Matteo Aimini, Reem Alharfush, Mounir Sabeh Affaki, Marco Ardielli, Maria-Thala Aswad, Marco Ballarin, Maria Antonia Barucco, Mattia Bertin, Viola Bertini, Serena Cominelli, Filippo De Dominicis, Fabián de la Fuente, Michele Di Marco, Silvia Dalzero, Lorenzo Fabian, Margherita Ferrari, Rania Mansour, Kindah Mousli, Renata Palladini, Ottavio Paponetti, Cristiana Pasquini, Luna Rajab, Giuseppe Ricupero, Fares Saleh, Alexis Schachter, Federico Tomasoni, Linda Zardo

THIS VOLUME WAS WRITTEN JOINTLY BY BENNO ALBRECHT AND JACOPO GALLI AND IS THE RESULT OF A CONTINUOUS PROCESS OF DIALOGUE AND PEER REVIEW. THE INTRODUCTION (PP. 12–15) CAN BE ATTRIBUTED TO BENNO ALBRECHT AND THE CHAPTERS 1, 2, 3, 4, 6 (PP. 16–135, 180–205) TO JACOPO GALLI. THE TEXTS IN CHAPTER 5 WERE WRITTEN BY ELISA VENDEMINI (VENEZIA, PP. 138–143), CHIARA SEMENZIN (LIMA, PP. 144–149), GIULIA PIACENTI (ALEPPO, PP. 150–155), SABRINA RIGHI (MOSUL, PP. 156–161), ANDREA FANTIN (NILE DELTA, PP. 162–167), SERENA PAPPALARDO (ACCRA, PP. 168–173), AND MARCO MARINO (IRPIN, PP. 174–179).

•

This book was made possible thanks to the support of:

Nohad Haj Salih – I.Barbon Shipping and Logistics

CITIES UNDER PRESS URE.

A DESIGN STRATEGY

FOR URBAN

RECONSTRUCTION

BENNO ALBRECHT / JACOPO GALLI

ARCHI TANGLE

TABLE OF CONTENTS

●

Introduction . 12

1. **GLOBAL CHALLENGES** . 24

1.1 The City in the Risk Society . 26
1.2 Urbicide and Violence . 28
1.3 Conflict Recurrence . 29
1.4 Disasters and Climate Change . 40
1.5 Social and Economic Risks . 46

2. **HISTORICAL EXPERIENCES** . 52

2.1 Reassessing Reconstruction . 54
2.2 Transformation Map . 55
2.3 Classifying Reconstruction . 60
2.4 Unprecedented Scale of Destruction . 76

3. **STRATEGY** . 80

3.1 Top Down / Bottom Up . 82
3.2 Cataclysmic Credit / Gradual Credit . 83
3.3 Layers / Cells . 88
3.4 Project / Process . 104
3.5 Reconstruction Laboratory . 105
3.6 Operational Phases . 108

4_ **SUSTAINABLE TRANSITION**   . 112

4_1   Exporting the Historical Core   . 114
4_2   The Leap Forward   . 115
4_3   Decentralized Model   . 121
4_4   Adaptive Circularity   . 124

5_ **EXPLORATIONS**   . 136

5_1   Settlement Principle as a Chance   . 138
      for Urban Metamorphosis / VENEZIA
5_2   Urban Triggers in Post-Earthquake   . 144
      Reconstruction / LIMA
5_3   The Reconstruction of Small Size / ALEPPO   . 150
5_4   Souks as Urban Catalysts / MOSUL   . 156
5_5   From Hazard to Opportunity: . 162
      The Controlled Flooding Strategy / NILE DELTA
5_6   Design without a Design / ACCRA   . 168
5_7   Piecemeal Planning at Work / IRPIN   . 174

6_ **DESIGN**   . 180

6_1   Urban Restoration   . 182
6_2   Urban Triggers   . 188
6_3   Backbones   . 190
6_4   Induced Design   . 196
6_5   Growing Evolutionary Mechanisms   . 200

Bibliography   . 206
Credits   . 216

BOOK+

USE THE QR CODE
TO ACCESS ADDITIONAL CONTENT
AND EXCLUSIVE MATERIAL

INTRODUCTION

•

CITIES UNDER PRESSURE presents a concrete idea for the sustainable reconstruction of cities and territories involved in extreme traumatic events. It illustrates a necessary paradigm shift from current intervention strategies, presenting a new approach that needs to be tested, scaled, and adapted, but one that can potentially be immediately applied in regions involved in events such as violent conflict, natural disaster, or major social distress. Cities Under Pressure is the result of a series of design and research experiences carried out by Urbicide Task Force, a think tank based at the Università Iuav di Venezia in Venice, Italy, that collaborates actively with major public and private stakeholders. The research and designs produced by the group have been presented at international conferences and workshops, published in peer-reviewed journals, and included in architectural exhibitions. This volume comprises six chapters, thirty-one subchapters, and one hundred and fifty figures. It lends itself to reading from start to finish or to just glancing at the figures, measuring dimensions with a ruler, or sketching over the pages, focusing solely on a single topic or looking carefully at each bibliographic entry. The text and the matching figures are intended to reflect a global approach that, with the proper adaptation mechanisms, can be applied anywhere. The visual and spatial variability of the presented urban designs demonstrates the open nature of the design approach, which is not a rigid set of rules but rather a system capable of fruitfully controlling a succession of countless decisions producing a multiplicity of variations.

The first chapter, "Global Challenges," describes how the risk society paradigm influences the built environment and categorizes the different pressures imposed on global cities. The second chapter, "Historical Experiences,"

INTRODUCTION

summarizes and classifies the various mechanisms that have been employed in reconstructions in the past, building a precious toolbox for future interventions. The third chapter, "Strategy," illustrates the overall process that will allow the definition of a reconstructed city with the highest possible qualitative and quantitative features, beauty, and performances. The fourth chapter, "Sustainable Transition," defines an alternative model of city-making based on a different use of available technology for maximizing the quality of life of communities. The fifth chapter, "Explorations," provides a set of examples of site-specific local projects that permit a stress test of the defined approach. The sixth and last chapter, "Design," aims to set in motion a complex mechanism to provide designers with the conceptual and operative tools that will allow us to bravely and successfully face cities under pressure.

Cities Under Pressure defines a strategy that hopefully will find multiple on-site applications, but it is first and foremost an attempt to trace the unstable borders of a design approach capable of facing the necessary paradigm shift imposed by the current global condition. The ambitious goal is to provide architects, urban planners, and design experts with a new perspective on the shaping of cities and territories, one that is capable of concretely representing the urgency of a transition toward a development model able to preserve the Earth and its current and future inhabitants. It is an intergenerational message sent into a foggy but foreseeable future with the strong belief that "in the end we will conserve only what we love; we will love only what we understand; and we will understand only what we are taught" (DIOUM 1968).

A MIDJOURNEY IN CITIES UNDER PRESSURE

●

Bits of images from the incessant media stream allow us to see glimpses of the cities under pressure paradigm: situations that highlight the contradictions and dystopias of current urban environments and anticipate upcoming scenarios. The images on the following pages were generated by the artificial intelligence program Midjourney starting from a selection of headlines from major media outlets. The results are situations that are, at the very same time, real and surreal, inspiring and frightening, surprising and plausible.

→. Yoga instructor Maksym Burlaka celebrates International Yoga Day in Kharkiv by doing a handstand next to an unexploded bomb. *Ukraine.ua*, June 21, 2022.

↑ . A hungry polar bear arrives
in industrial Norilsk after
walking 1,500 kilometers
inland in search of food.
The Siberian Times, June 17,
2019.

← . Flying cattle class: Qatar
to airlift 4,000 cows to break
Saudi Arabia-led blockade.
Middle East Eye, June 13, 2017.

← . Influencer is facing
a barrage of criticism for
publishing before her 700,000
followers an image that turns
the riots in Barcelona into a
fashion editorial.
El Pais, October 17, 2019.

→ . China tears down tower
blocks an effort to boost the
stalling economy.
Beijing has adopted a "build,
pause, demolish, repeat"
strategy. *The Telegraph*,
August 23, 2022.

A MIDJOURNEY IN CITIES UNDER PRESSURE

→ . Ukrainian brewery ditches beer to make Russian-fighting Molotov cocktails instead. *The Washington Post*, February 25, 2022.

← . Newly wed Syrian couple have their wedding pictures taken in front of a heavily damaged building. *The Guardian,* February 5, 2016.

← . Chanel's spring fashion show takes place in a field of wind turbines. Eco-chic has definitely arrived. Will it do anything to change the world? *Grist*, October 8, 2012.

A MIDJOURNEY IN CITIES UNDER PRESSURE

↑ . Humiliated Venice:
November 12, the apocalypse
of the submerged city.
Il Gazzettino, November 12,
2019.

←. Amazon will open a
$21 million state-of-the
art warehouse in Tijuana,
Mexico, that abuts a housing
settlement made of cardboard,
tarp, and wood scraps.
Vice News, September 7, 2021.

←. Hundreds of migrants,
mostly Afghans, were brutally
expelled from Place de la
République in Paris.
Le Monde, November 24,
2020.

←. Las Vegas places homeless
people in a parking lot,
6 feet apart, while casinos are
deserted and thousands
of hotel rooms are empty.
The New York Times, March
31, 2020.

A MIDJOURNEY IN CITIES UNDER PRESSURE

←. Heatherwick's
Vessel closes again after
fourth suicide.
Deezen, August 2, 2021.

←. Homeless Pacoima
man creates a decorative
encampment.
San Fernando Valley Sun / El Sol,
June 23, 2021.

←. Dozens of protesters jump
in the swimming pool of the
Presidential Palace in Baghdad
to face Iraq's hot weather.
Iraqi News, August 29, 2022.

A MIDJOURNEY IN CITIES UNDER PRESSURE

↓. 22-year-old engineering student Alaa Salah chanting in front of a crowd of protesters in Sudan.
Al Jazeera, May 4, 2019.

A MIDJOURNEY IN CITIES UNDER PRESSURE

1. GLOBAL CHALLENGES

GLOBAL CHALLENGES

The global risk society paradigm describes a world in which the concept of risk has broken all kinds of borders and extended to the daily life of millions of people, even threatening the very existence of humanity as a whole. This scenario has immediate and unexplored consequences for urban environments: an increase in traumatic events, but also a strong influence on social and economic processes that continuously shape cities and territories. Urbicide and widespread violence, disasters and climate change, social and economic risks are currently absent from urban discourse but have the potential to become extraordinary engines of urban metamorphosis. Extreme events have to be seen as a chance to liberate the potential inherent in every radical transformation mechanism and to explore disruptive solutions.

GLOBAL CHALLENGES

●

1.1   THE CITY IN THE RISK SOCIETY

Historical evolution and processes of cultural and economic globalization have brought out relevant and frightening risks on a global scale: from climate change to uncontrolled urban explosion, from the spread of informal low-intensity conflicts to the development of extended forms of technological control and the enormous widening of economic and social inequalities. Humanity as a whole is today facing epochal challenges that require a radical metamorphosis of inhabited spaces. We live in what Ulrich Beck has defined as a global risk society:

> the speeding up of modernisation has produced a gulf between the world of quantifiable risk, in which we think and act, and the world of non-quantifiable insecurities that we are creating . . . . "Risk" inherently contains a concept of control. Pre-modern dangers were attributed to nature, gods and demons. Risk is a modern concept. It presumes decision-making. As soon as we speak in terms of "risk," we are talking about calculating the incalculable, colonising the future . . . . But what happens in world risk society is that we enter a world of uncontrollable risk and we don't even have a language to describe what we are facing. "Uncontrollable risk" is a contradiction in terms. And yet it is the only apt description for the second-order, unnatural, human-made, manufactured uncertainties and hazards beyond boundaries (BECK 2002).

The responses to this condition of permanent existential siege, which undermines the very reasons of community living and suggests an imminent "end of time," have been compared by Slavoj Žižek to the five stages of mourning: rejection, anger, negotiation, depression, acceptance (ŽIŽEK 2011). Today's reactions are technocratic, convinced of the salvific function of markets and technological innovations, or depressed, in the total lack of future prospects, or even apocalyptic, aimed at strengthening the individualism of "save whoever can" (LEONARDI AND BARBERO 2017). Resignation appears as one (and often the only) possible outcome of unacceptable inequalities, of catastrophic natural phenomena, of the irreparable loss of biodiversity, but it is not necessary: the challenges hide a new revolutionary space for the convergence of the different struggles and for the creation of a common front [KLEIN 2014]. It is necessary to build "not sad philosophies about change" [GIANNUZZI 2015] that abandon the sense of inevitability and instead allow renewed political, social, and behavioral choices and, most of all, a renewed design attitude. Beck too underlines the extraordinary opportunities for the radical rethinking of the approaches and processes that shape our societies and cities, within the paradigm of the global risk society. "Uncontrollable risk is now irredeemable and deeply engineered into all the processes that sustain life in advanced societies. Pessimism then seems to be the only rational stance. But this is a one-sided and therefore truly misguided view. It ignores the new terrain. It is dwarfed by the sheer scale of the new opportunities opened up by today's threats, that is the axis of conflicts in world risk society" [BECK 2002].

For the purposes of this study, we have subdivided these risks and opportunities into three categories in an attempt to systematize the types of extreme events that deeply influence urban metamorphosis in the contemporary built environment. The three proposed categories are:

a.
URBICIDE AND VIOLENCE

Currently wars vary in scope, dimension, cause, and involved actors, while terrorism and political violence extend the frontier of conflict possibilities to the whole globe, and violent acts can rapidly involve areas peaceful until just very recently.

b.
DISASTERS AND CLIMATE CHANGE

Natural disasters (earthquakes, floods, fires, etc.) impact, at various levels of risk, large areas of the planet, while the early effects of climate change and biodiversity loss significantly increase the scope of danger and extend the percentage of population involved.

c.
SOCIAL AND ECONOMIC RISKS

The enlarging of global and local inequalities has substantially increased the exposure to risk of large strata of the population, in both developed and developing areas. Social and economic processes can have a catastrophic impact on urban environments and territories.

1_ GLOBAL CHALLENGES

This vertical subdivision of interrelated elements partially fails in describing the interwoven nature of the different issues that can as well be read in a horizontal manner (blue wars, climate inequality, ethnic and religious wars, etc.). However, the vertical simplification permits a definition of clear categories that, while not to be seen as rigid borders, can act as useful elements for the interpretation of events and influence the development of design strategies.

1_2   **URBICIDE AND VIOLENCE**

Today, we are faced with a creeping Third World War, or something similar to a global civil war: permanent, unconventional, asymmetrical, local, and mobile, but with major consequences and reverberations. We are witnessing a substantial change in the form of conflict, or of perpetual non-peace, which sees a progressive increase in the involvement of civilians, both victims and targets, compared to the past. The consequence is that cities have become the preferred battlefields, and their destruction, via ground or air, has become a primary strategic goal for military and political purposes [GRAHAM 2010].

This condition leads to the reemergence of the term "urbicide" in urban discourse, defined as the deliberate violence against cities, their destruction, and the intentional elimination of a collective "memory made of stone." Today, war is fought in urban contexts, and "urbicide is a form of genocide, the fundamentally illegitimate form of modern war in which a civilian population as such is targeted for destruction by armed force" [SHAW 2004]. The term urbicide was popularized by Marshall Berman to describe the consequences on his native Bronx of Robert Moses's "meat axe" in the 1960s [CARO 1974] and first applied to a war context in the 1990s during the Yugoslav Wars [BOGDANOVIC 1993] with the exhibition *Mostar 92 Urbicid* [RIBAREVIC-NIKOLIC AND JURIC 1992] and a seminal article by Giancarlo De Carlo in *Spazio e Società* [DE CARLO 1997]. Today, the dire images coming from Aleppo, Benghazi, Sanaa, or Kyiv show the consequences of combat action involving the heart and souls of cities on the population and on the urban environment.

Urbicide is the silent witnessing of the complete integration of the military–industrial complex [HOSSEIN-ZADEH 2006] and the tip of the iceberg of a global trend toward the widespread use of military tools to confront urban issues. It is the conscious transformation of military operations into military urbanism: "techniques of urban militarism and urbicidal violence serve to discipline or displace dissent and resistance. They erase or delegitimize urban claims and spaces that stand in the way of increasing predatory forms of urban planning that clear the way for super-modern infrastructure, production centres or enclaves for urban consumption" [GRAHAM 2010]. Current conflicts can be defined as cosmopolitan wars: low-intensity, mobile, permanent, unconventional, and timeless conflict. These are wars fought on a large scale, which see national and transnational armies and coalitions, terrorist groups, armed groups, guerrilla formations, and ethnic, religious, political, and ideological militias as contingent realities. Such actors associate and dissociate themselves depending on their immediate interests, on the global geopolitical situation, and on various ideological nuances, simultaneously fighting on several fronts according to strategic factors of momentary interest. From this perspective, weapons and battlefields undergo a process of radical cosmopolitanization (HIPPLER 2014). Technological and cybernetic support, local or global terrorism, online indoctrinations, regional and continental migratory processes, media management and "spectacularization" of terror, manipulation of risk perception, and attempts to influence leaders and electoral bodies are all new fighting weapons.

The new paradigm can be defined as "war amongst the people" (SMITH 2005): a struggle that is fought less and less on traditional battlegrounds, and increasingly in places and through forms that make it impossible to immediately identify the expected results of each participant. It is not a *Volkskrieg* (the war of the people theorized by Carl von Clausewitz as a response to massive foreign invasion); not a heroic confrontation in which the people, as a single body, become a belligerent force. It is a war that is essentially fought in the midst of the people and using the people as a weapon. Sarah Sewall, author of the counterinsurgency manual for the US Army, describes the new soldier as a social worker, an urbanist, an anthropologist, and a psychologist (SEWALL 2007); "rather than a giant computer game, modern wars turned out to be more like social work with guns" (BACEVICH 2009).

1.3 CONFLICT RECURRENCE

Ninety percent of the wars of the twenty-first century's first decade occurred in countries that had experienced civil war in the prior thirty years. Conflicts have become a recurring event involving certain territories with a given return period, almost like a natural catastrophe. Selected areas of the globe have become the global testing ground for necropolitics (MBEMBE 2003), the physical space in which death, its presence and its possibility, has become a permanent feature of the life of the majority of the population. Conflict recurrence generates a new type of war: one with no easily defined front lines and rarely a clear beginning or end that shifts fluidly in time and place, evolving unpredictably with sudden changes in alignment and power distribution. State and non-state actors from within and across borders are driven in the conflicts by fractured interests such as personal and collective identities, control of local resources, and strategic, economic, and ideological competition; adding fuel to long-standing grievances and tearing communities apart (WORLD BANK 2011, 2017).

URBICIDE / 1936–2023

London / GBR 1941

Rotterdam / NLD 1940

Aachen / NLD 1944

Le Havre / FRA 1944

Orléans / FRA 1944

Lyon / FRA 1944

Gdansk / POL 1945

Wroclaw / POL 1945

Dresden / DEU 1945

Wien / AUT 1945

URBICIDE / 1936–2023

←

The dimension of each triangle represents the total population of the city in the year before the conflict, while the darker portion is the percentage of the urban environment that was completely destroyed. The map constructs an asynchronous vision of urbicide, comparing cities destroyed in different time frames, from World War II to recent conflicts in Syria and Ukraine, highlighting the substantial increase in the average size of involved cities and in the total scope of destruction.

The data visualization allows one to understand the global trend of urban warfare and the increase in average size of destroyed cities. Cities destroyed in World War II were mainly of a small size (with substantial exceptions such as Berlin, London, Tokyo, Warsaw, etc.), while urbicide experienced a stable decrease in the second half of the twentieth century, only to increase again in the new millennium when the incremental growth of urban population brought conflict back to densely populated areas (Aleppo, Mosul, Kyiv, etc.).

1_ GLOBAL CHALLENGES

_ Population
_ Destruction %
_ Location / Year

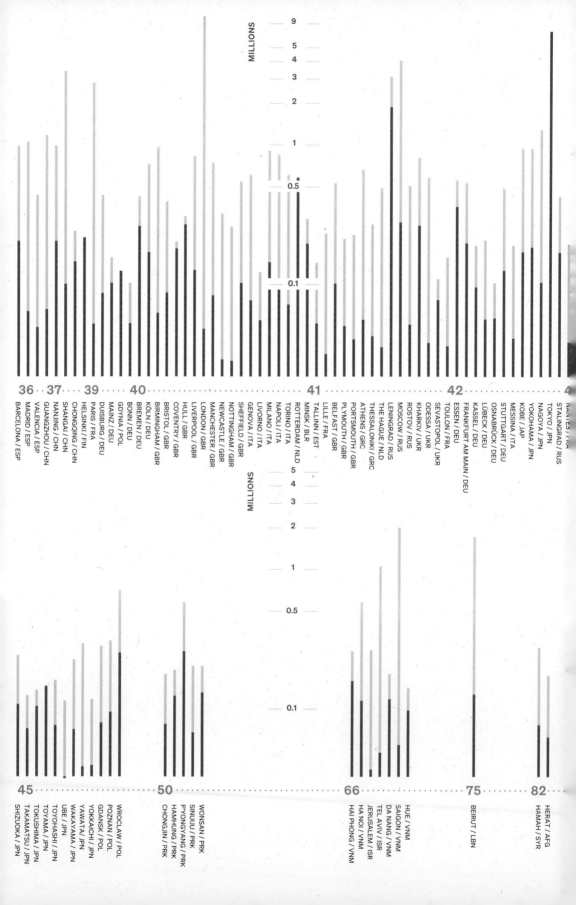

MILLIONS

9
5
4
3
2

1

0.5

0.1

36 · · 37 · · · 39 · · · 40

BARCELONA / ESP
MADRID / ESP
VALENCIA / ESP
GUANGZHOU / CHN
NANJING / CHN
SHANGAI / CHN
CHONGQING / CHN
HELSINKI / FIN
PARIS / FRA
DUISBURG / DEU
MAINZ / DEU
GDYNIA / POL
BONN / DEU
BREMEN / DEU
BIRMINGHAM / GBR
BRISTOL / GBR
COVENTRY / GBR
HULL / GBR
LIVERPOOL / GBR
LONDON / GBR
MANCHESTER / GBR
NEWCASTLE / GBR
NOTTINGHAM / GBR
SHEFFIELD / GBR
GENOVA / ITA
LIVORNO / ITA
MILANO / ITA
NAPOLI / ITA
TORINO / ITA
ROTTERDAM / NLD
MINSK / BLR
TALLINN / EST
LILLE / FRA
BELFAST / GBR
PLYMOUTH / GBR
PORTSMOUTH / GBR
ATHENS / GRC
THESSALONIKI / GRC
THE HAGUE / NLD
LENINGRAD / RUS
MOSCOW / RUS
ROSTOV / RUS
KHARKIV / UKR
ODESSA / UKR
SEVASTOPOL / UKR
TOULON / FRA
ESSEN / DEU
FRANKFURT AM MAIN / DEU
KASSEL / DEU
LÜBECK / DEU
OSNABRÜCK / DEU
STUTTGART / DEU
MESSINA / ITA
KOBE / JAP
YOKOHAMA / JPN
NAGOYA / JPN
TOKYO / JPN
STALINGRAD / RUS

41

42

4

NAPLES / ITA

MILLIONS

5
4
3
2

1

0.5

0.1

45 · · · · 50

BARCELONA / ESP
SHIZUOKA / JPN
TAKAMATSU / JPN
TOKUSHIMA / JPN
TOYAMA / JPN
UBE / JPN
WAKAYAMA / JPN
YAWATA / JPN
YOKKAICHI / JPN
GDANSK / POL
POZNAN / POL
WROCLAW / POL
TOYOHASHI / JPN

66

75

82

CHONGJIN / PRK
HAMHUNG / PRK
PYONGYANG / PRK
SINUIJU / PRK
WONSAN / PRK

HAI PHONG / VNM
HA NOI / VNM
JERUSALEM / ISR
TEL AVIV / ISR
DA NANG / VNM
SAIGON / VNM
HUE / VNM

BEIRUT / LBN

HERAT / AFG
HAMAH / SYR

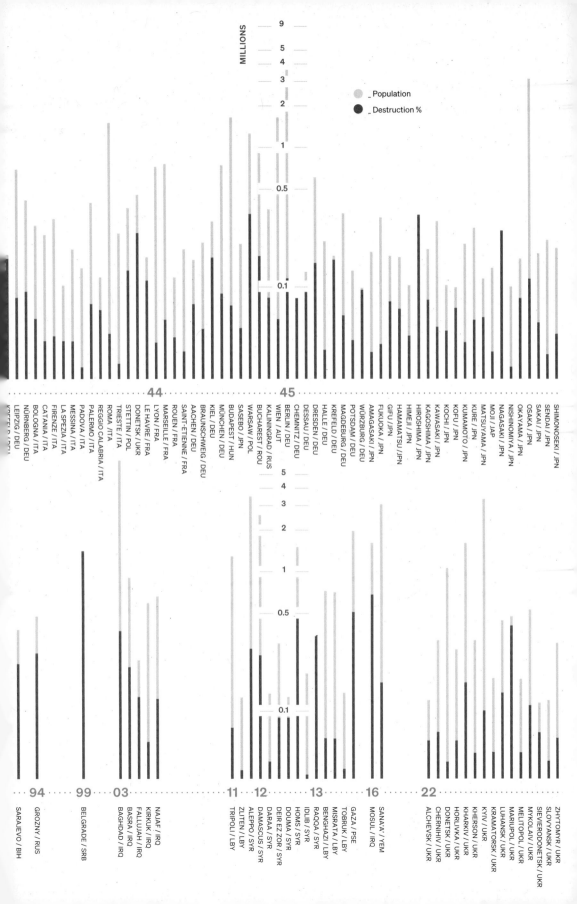

VIOLENCE / 2018-2021

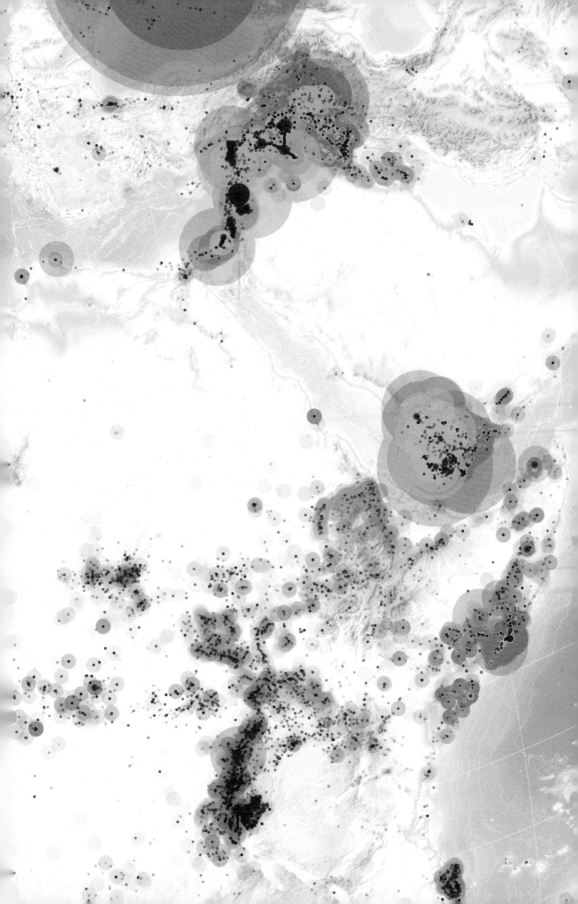

VIOLENCE / 2018–2021

→

Each point on the map represents a violent event. The color and the dimension of each circle respectively denote the type of event and the frequency of violence. Additionally, the gradient color opacity is the selected time frame.

The types of events shown are: battles, violent clashes between at least two state or non-state armed groups; explosions or remote violence, explosive devices used to engage in conflict, either one-sided or from both sides; violence against civilians, attacks on unarmed civilians including sexual violence, abduction, and forced disappearance.

1_ GLOBAL CHALLENGES

_ Violence

_ Explosions

_ Battles

Kampala / UGA

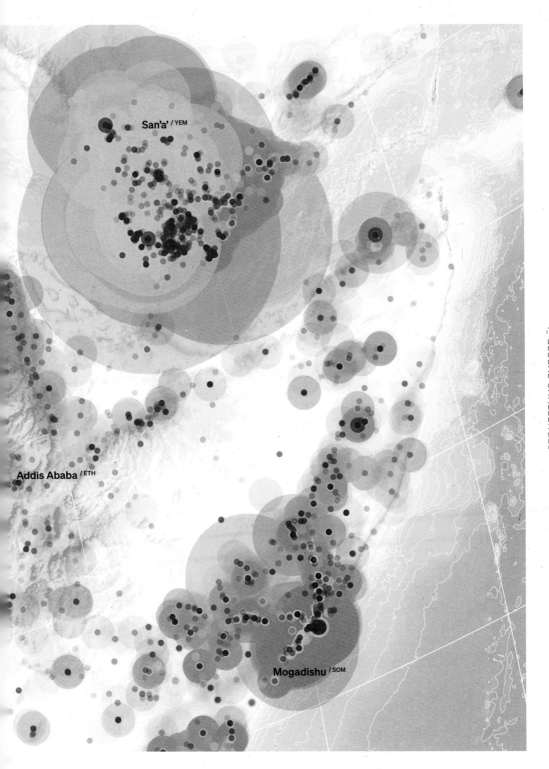

San'a' / YEM

Addis Ababa / ETH

Mogadishu / SOM

Today's conflicts can be characterized as *fluid* in their unpredictable evolution, *fractured* across space and across multiple actors and interests, and *informal* in their socioeconomic consequences. *Fluid* wars evolve unpredictably and recur continuously: local and national communities are broken, social cohesion is undermined, generations are lost, and social capital is depleted. Wars are *fractured* across space, actors, and interests; even when prolonged conflicts are localized in defined parts of a country, they also have regional and international spillover that causes violence, illicit undertakings, and businesses to flourish domestically and regionally. *Informal* conflicts generate unexpected economic and political underpinnings; relationships are often reconfigured as conflict fuels informal activities and exchange both within and across borders; informality prompts workforce changes and reorientation of the political economy in war-torn societies and in neighboring countries. For war-torn societies to move toward sustainable peace, the root causes of their conflicts must be understood and carefully addressed. Previous peace-building efforts and reconstruction experiences failed to avoid a relapse into conflict and violence: "Traditional efforts usually adopted a bricks-and-mortar and state-centered approach focused on rebuilding physical assets and central institutions, temporarily restoring the country on the surface. But by overlooking or failing to address, and even repressing, deeper social, political, and economic tensions, the real drivers of conflict, they sometimes made the eventual relapse all the more violent. Such reconstructions could lock the country into a 'conflict trap'" [WORLD BANK 2020].

Only a good reconstruction, one able to provide solutions for the immediate necessities of populations exhausted by war and at the same time able to contrast the systemic reasons for violence [ISMAIL 2018] can arrest the vicious circle of conflict recurrence. We need a new design strategy that sees the reshaping of territories and urban environments as a tool for peace, a strategy able to comprehend and interact with the sum of intertwined societal, economic, and urban problems. Reconstruction should consider the initiation of positive economic cycles and promote a transition toward sustainable solutions in terms of technological performance and community participation. Fluid, fractured, and informal conflict requires sensible design interventions capable of being a seismograph of past, present, and future needs, threats, and hopes.

1.4 DISASTERS AND CLIMATE CHANGE

The *Cities Under Pressure* design strategy operates in a framework that considers climate change as an already occurred catastrophe, leading to the necessity of developing completely new conceptual and operative models. Climatic experts widely already operate under this assumption, but urban design and emergency experts still consider the phenomenon to be a recurring series of crises and propose punctual solutions that fail to interpret and react to the complex set of global and local consequences. We need to assume that ongoing climate change is a macro-catastrophe which moves the current stable system toward a future system that is unexpected (but designable). We can in fact define climate change as the process by which environmental standards, defined in terms of rainfall, temperature, and correlated effects (among which disasters are only the most visible and extreme manifestations), are transforming our urban systems with an increasing impact that is in part recognizable but not fully forecastable in a comprehensive vision.

Current studies on climate change adaptation and disaster risk reduction lack cross references; despite clear overlaps the two disciplines and research communities rarely speak to one another or share methods, languages, and results [FORINO ET AL. 2015; BERTIN ET AL. 2020]. Disaster risk reduction experts largely concentrate on vulnerabilities and risks in specific areas connected to single events [BIRKMANN AND TEICHMANN 2010]. Climate change experts, on the other hand, have a longer-term vision, guided by an awareness that the current urban model will need to be radically rethought due to climate evolution, but, at the same time, they lack consolidated design and planning skills [GALLOPIN 2006; ISENHOUR ET AL. 2015] and often fail to understand the complex factors (economic, social, spatial, etc.) that define urban environments. The *Cities Under Pressure* strategy rethinks the relationship between the two communities, imagining a new, integrated approach that recognizes ongoing climate change in relationship with the traditional skills of emergency management [RAMROTH 2007]. Disaster risk management must today acknowledge the different and increasingly frequent catastrophic events as manifestations of a single overall phenomenon and, consequently, rethink its operating design and planning methods [AQUILUÉ 2021; SANDERSON ET AL. 2016] on the basis of a persistent and already ongoing event, rather than on a multitude of partial, episodic ones. Considering climate change as a global catastrophe means considering urban spaces as systems in transition, in which every part of life is affected by changes that need to be taken into account immediately.

In order to face climate change as an ongoing global emergency resulting from a catastrophe that has already occurred, we must rethink how and when design and planning tools are produced, revised, adapted, and applied on site. Climate change must immediately be seen as a "civilisational wake-up call" [KLEIN 2014] toward the definition of a renewed design paradigm capable of controlling and shaping the Anthropocene [CRUTZEN 2006; MCNEILL AND ENGELKE 2014], the geological era where humans are the engine of the modification (and even the possible destruction) of the planet. *Cities Under Pressure* assumes the Anthropocene paradigm and immediately further criticizes the concept through the notion of the Capitalocene [MOORE 2016], which sees financial capital as the main shaper of the built environment; and introduces climate justice [ROBINSON 2018] as a factor that binds together inextricably linked climatic, social, and economic risks. Designing in and for the Capitalocene means considering contemporary—as tools and as ultimate goals—the power relations that have historically shaped socioecological relations, "avoiding misplacing together exploited and exploiters, colonised and colonisers, bombed and bombers, subordinates and dominant, expropriated and expropriators" [AVALLONE 2017].

1_ GLOBAL CHALLENGES

DISASTERS / 2020-2021

Haldwani / IND

Katmandu

Rajkot / IND

Hazaribag / IND

Yavatmal / IND

Panaji, Goa / IND

Kadapa / IND

Bharua Khali / BGD

Pyinbongyi / MMR

DISASTERS / 2020-2021

←

The map overlaps hydrological disasters, primarily focusing on flood hazards by combining coastal floods, flash floods, ice jam floods, and riverine floods.

The events are represented in terms of risk, overall affected area, and death ratio of each event. The orange gradient represents flood mortality risk from a low to extreme level (vivid orange color), the red gradient refers to the areas affected by flood events registered during the years 2020 and 2021, while the white diamond shape and its size identify the death ratio for each event.

1_ GLOBAL CHALLENGES

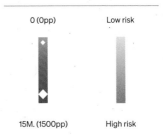

0 (0pp)   Low risk

15M. (1500pp)   High risk

1_5 SOCIAL AND ECONOMIC RISKS

Although conflict and climate change have the most immediately visible consequences on urban environments, immaterial social and economic processes are the
true shapers of contemporary cities and territories (SECCHI 2013). Today, the only active
engine of urban change on a global scale is the real-estate state (STEIN 2019); the transformation of urban spaces and functions into financial commodities has turned cities into the cornerstone of global economic growth. The total value of global real
estate is 217 billion dollars, thirty-six times the value of all gold ever mined on the
planet; real estate accounts for 60 percent of global financial resources, and 75 percent of world wealth is represented by the value of homes. Capital has definitively
transformed itself into the only possible urban form factor, making the work of architects and planners totally ancillary to decision-making processes.

The real-estate state has led to an unprecedented rise in inequality at global, regional, and city levels (MILANOVIĆ 2016). Immense concentrations of wealth, privilege, and
consumerism can be observed in all global cities, side by side with an exploding "planet
of slums" (DAVIS 2005). The current global coronavirus pandemic (BLAKELEY 2020) has only made
evident an ongoing process of urban and global imbalance: "the 'covid-event' comes to
lift the veil and puts the deep systemic dyscrasia we live in under the eyes of all, dyscrasia that was not caused by the virus: it was already there, but we could no longer grasp
it. It can be described as the distance between the needs of capital and those of humans
(and of other living beings, and of the earth)" (CONSIGLIERE AND ZAVARONI 2020).

The first reaction to these conditions is a renewed interest in the theme
of urban commons (OSTROM 1990; HESS AND OSTROM 2007), which has led to the creation of movements that seek to communalize many functions, today in public or private hands
(PUTNAM 2000; BANERJEE AND DUFLO 2011), in order to access socially rather than individually produced wealth (DE ANGELIS 2017). The shared management of commons can become possible through a rich mix of instrumentalities (HARVEY 2012) that is not given but needs
to be constructed through the rethinking of living practices, first and foremost the
process of city-making. Despite these early forms of resistance, current cities and
territories are still plagued by enormous social, economic, and political challenges
that significantly alter the processes of urban metamorphosis and often prevent a
serious transition toward a sustainable development model. Economic exclusion is
today the main shaper of global urban environments, and the imbalance in income
among different neighborhoods of global cities has become similar to the disparity
between different countries, leading to gated communities (BAGAEEN AND UDUKU 2012) and
triggering securitarian policies in which military urbanism techniques are applied
to apparently peaceful environments (KRIPA AND MUELLER 2021).

Inequality often leads to social segregation, which mixes with ethnic, religious, or social factors to force an undesirable population [AGIER 2011] to stay within rigid urban borders [ZETTER AND BOANO 2010], ghettos, enclaves, refugee camps, or in the infinite favelas, *villas miseria*, bidonvilles, or shantytowns that account for a staggering 24 percent of the global population. Spaces for dialogue and participation are limited, thus leading to recurring political demonstrations by neglected strata of the population, and to counter repression techniques that alter public spaces temporarily or permanently [RABBAT 2012; MOSTAFAVI 2017].

The sum of conflicts, disasters, climate change, and social and economic issues paints a difficult scenario for "our common future" [BRUNDTLAND 1987] and calls for a transition to new models capable of transforming this overwhelming sum of pressures into design factors. Urban settlements are at the center stage of such a transition, being at the same time the areas most responsible for the current risks (70 percent of global emissions, 50 million urban inhabitants involved in war, a projected 216 million climate migrants), those benefitting from the current paradigm (50 percent of the global GDP comes from 380 cities, 83 percent of scientific products and patents), those more involved by future modifications (sea level rise alone will threaten 800 million people by 2050), and are, quite possibly, a significant part of the solution. *Cities Under Pressure* illustrates an open design strategy for intervention in cities and territories, an adaptable and sensible approach that indicates a possible path toward a transition capable of guaranteeing safety and well-being to a large majority of the global population.

1_ GLOBAL CHALLENGES

INEQUALITY / 2009-2019

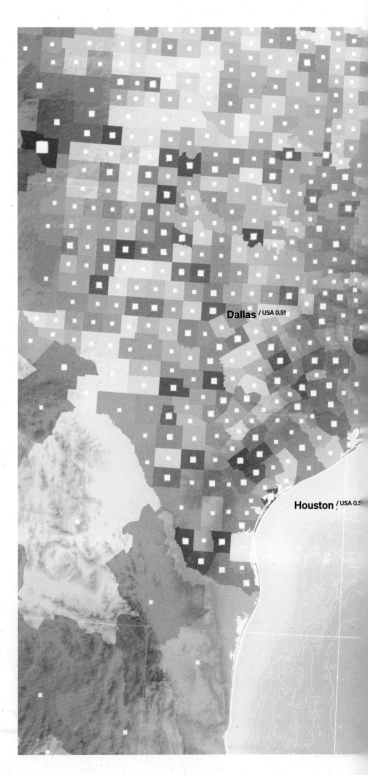

INEQUALITY / 2009–2019
→

The color gradient and size
of the square represent the
Gini coefficient at the federal,
regional, or county scale.

The Gini coefficient is an index
for the degree of inequality in
the distribution of income and
wealth, used to estimate how far
the income distribution deviates
from an equal distribution, where
0 expresses perfect equality and
1 maximum inequality.

A Gini coefficient above 0.4
is frequently associated with
political instability and growing
social tension.

Dallas / USA 0.51

Houston / USA 0.5

0.25

0.80

1_ GLOBAL CHALLENGES

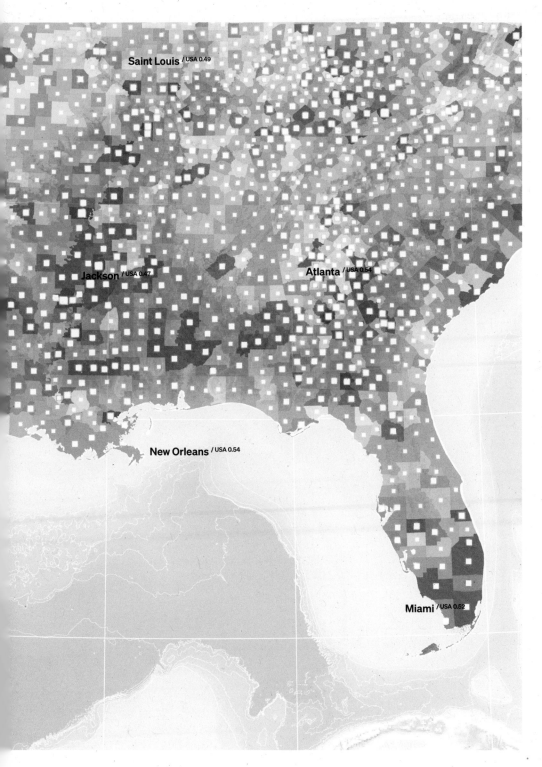

Saint Louis / USA 0.49

Jackson / USA 0.47

Atlanta / USA 0.54

New Orleans / USA 0.54

Miami / USA 0.52

2.

2_ HISTORICAL EXPERIENCES

HISTORICAL EXPERIENCES

The role played by extreme events in the initiation of trial-and-error processes characterizing the development of urban models has often been underestimated. Destruction and reconstruction have been extraordinary experimental chances, but an ordered tale of the different strategies and solutions tested has yet to be fully told. The critical redrawing of the most relevant case studies, and the comparative analyses of the processes in quantitative and qualitative terms, can initiate a necessary research effort to explore which (and how) past solutions can still be valuable benchmarks for the future. Only one certainty emerges: the unprecedented scale of current phenomena calls for innovative solutions capable of actualizing the lessons from the past.

HISTORICAL EXPERIENCES

●

2_1   REASSESSING RECONSTRUCTION

All Saints' Day in the year 1755 marked a ridge in urban history: the great city of Lisbon, Portugal, one of the global metropolises of its era, was completely destroyed by an earthquake and the resulting tsunami [SHRADY 2008]. The terror generated by the event would deeply influence the most important thinkers of the time: Voltaire dedicated a key chapter of his masterpiece *Candide* to it, Jean-Jacques Rousseau used it as an anti-urban argument against the concentration of population in cities, while Immanuel Kant published three books on the subject, marking the establishment of scientific geography. The cataclysm left centuries-long traces in European science, social life, religion, and philosophy: cities could face complete annihilation at any given moment, so the design and planning community needed to develop systems for prevention and reconstruction. Over 150 years later, at the end of World War I, the biologist and urbanist Patrick Geddes would call for the establishment of a "science and art of reconstruction" in his book *Ideas at War* [GEDDES AND SLATER 1917]. Despite the increasing number of cities destroyed by war and natural disaster in the long twentieth century, this cry was to remain unheard: while the field of emergency developed clear operational frameworks and dedicated institutions, reconstruction has never been able to fully become an independent discipline and remains subdivided among multiple experts and across different fields of study.

Nevertheless, it is worth noting how destruction has become a stable presence in architectural and urban discourse: "the twentieth century turned out to be the most destructive in human history. Between 1914 and 1970 especially, physical damage to the built environment was enlarged, dispersed and routinised so far and wide that it became a new architectural category in the public imagination, and an unavoidable datum of global historical thought" [ALLAIS 2018]. The importance given to issues of destruction is clearly shown by the relevant bibliography, which in recent years has been devoted to the subject of reconstruction, with a focus shifting from the construction of a historical perspective [HIPPLER 2014] to the issue of cultural identity and heritage preservation [BEVAN 2006;

BOLD ET AL. 2017; ALLAIS 2018); from geopolitical and economic reverberations (COWARD 2004; IKLÉ 2005) to the use of ICT tools for investigative purposes (WEIZMAN 2011, 2018), and to military tactics adapted to urban planning (PORTEOUS AND SMITH 2001; FRANKE 2003). In the field of urban studies, extensive research (mainly devoted to post–World War II Europe) has attempted to construct an organized history of reconstruction processes (MAMOLI AND TREBBI 1988; DIEFENDORF 1990; COGATO-LANZA AND BONIFAZIO 2009; JOHNSON-MARSHALL 2010; COHEN 2011; DÜWEL AND GUTSCHOW, 2013; MORAVÁNSZKY 2016) and to explore the different design approaches in terms of urban and architectural strategies (VALE AND CAMPANELLA 2005). Despite this massive research effort, a work capable of identifying and establishing a scientific approach able to describe and evaluate the different types of urban metamorphosis following extreme events is still missing. In order to begin the difficult process toward the establishment of a "discipline of reconstruction," we desperately need to construct the lenses through which to read past and current dynamics.

2_2   TRANSFORMATION MAP

The analyses of urban metamorphosis caused by destruction and reconstruction, carried out through critical redrawing, has never been conducted in a systematic way. In order to fill this relevant void in literature, we have rediscovered, actualized, and applied a representation method for the description of urban transformation as defined by Leonardo Benevolo (BENEVOLO 1971, 1991) in both his history books and his urban designs. By applying this same method to a large group of case studies, it is possible to build a framework for understanding urban metamorphosis that avoids hasty classification into rigid categories and instead allows the wide range of micro-variations and chances to emerge. Retracing the transformations not only allows one to witness past experiences but also builds an operational tool for understanding today's urban dynamics, with the final aim of orienting future intervention strategies, which permits a stratification of knowledge.

> It is a question of relocating architecture among the components of daily life, as a technique for juggling the limitations of space and time, fully comparable with all the others and already containing within it the reason for an extraordinary responsibility: the long duration of its artefacts with the multiplicity of relations that they entail (BENEVOLO 1988).

This type of analytical approach is defined by Benevolo as a screenplay of physical transformation, where architectural projects or urban environments are described and defined through all the specific characteristics of the object and its context, as would happen in a screenplay for a film or a theatrical production. The most important screenplay written and drawn by Benevolo is the illustration of the design processes that led to the current configuration of Piazza San Pietro in Rome, presented in *Casabella* no. 572 in 1990 (BENEVOLO 1990). His screenplay identifies three key moments in the history of the

2_ HISTORICAL EXPERIENCES

TRANSFORMATION
MAP

DRESDEN
●

On February 13 and 15, 1945, the city of Dresden, Germany, known as the Florence of the Elbe, was heavily damaged by four allied raids. The city was famous for its extraordinary baroque monuments, such as the Zwinger and the Frauenkirche, ensconced in a dense and cohesive urban pattern of raw houses defined by the controlled application of strict building regulations. The Allied bombing and the subsequent neglect by the postwar German

DRESDEN / DEU 1945

Destruction map. Destroyed and preserved buildings.

2_ HISTORICAL EXPERIENCES

Democratic Republic (GDR) government, which restored only a few selected buildings, led to an overall state of abandonment of the historical core. In 1989, with the end of the Soviet era, the city reinitiated the reconstruction process, which symbolically terminated with the second inauguration of the Frauenkirche in 2005. The transformation map shows the complex entanglement of temporal and spatial layers, with damaged buildings immediately restored after the war, others rebuilt over a longer time frame on the same site and in the same way, and a complete alteration of the minor urban texture around the monuments, with new building types.

DRESDEN / DEU 2005

Reconstruction map. Preserved and reconstructed buildings.

2_ HISTORICAL EXPERIENCES

● _ Preserved buildings

○ _ Destroyed buildings

● _ Reconstructed buildings

▨ _ Reconstruction on destruction

DRESDEN / DEU 1945-2005

Transformation map. Destroyed, preserved, and reconstructed buildings.

A. Destroyed and reconstructed buildings. Reconstruction on the previous building footprint.

B. Preserved buildings. Consolidation works.

C. Destroyed and unreconstructed buildings. Non-reconstruction.

D. New buildings. New reconstruction outside the previous footprint.

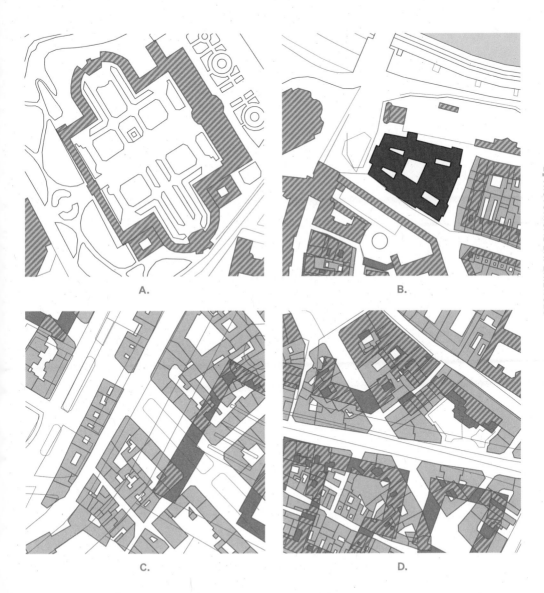

A.

B.

C.

D.

2_ HISTORICAL EXPERIENCES

urban complex: the condition of the square before Bernini's project, the completion of the colonnade with parallel arms and the definition of the ovoid square by Bernini between 1662 and 1670, and the current conditions following the demolition of the Spina dei Borghi and the construction of Via della Conciliazione on a project by Marcello Piacentini and Attilio Spaccarelli completed between 1937 and 1950 (BENEVOLO 2004). The three phases are not only described and documented but also drawn at the same scale and with the same type of representation in order to eliminate any discrepancies given by the different drawing styles. The method of analysis allows one to understand the reasoning behind each design choice that cannot be explained through a simple observation of the current state.

The final drawing proposed in *Casabella* is the key element of the analysis, the transformation map: it superimposes the conditions before Piacentini's intervention onto the current one and shows with only three layers the complex intertwining of urban continuities and interruptions. The drawing has only three colors: red buildings are unchanged during the two periods, yellow ones are demolished, and blue ones reconstructed; yellow and blue dashed shows the structures rebuilt in a previously occupied area. The sum of these temporal and spatial layers is a powerful tool for the understanding of urban metamorphosis. Time becomes a design factor like space, and the representation of the different intervals contributes to the understanding of the evolutionary process, but above all of the visible structure, which is only the current concretization of complex phenomena that could, and still can, radically change the urban environment. The transformation map tool identified by Benevolo was applied to a series of case studies encompassing different types of extreme events. The systematic drafting of transformation maps makes it possible to compare the spatial consequences on the urban fabric of the various pressures and of reconstruction strategies. The transformation map, and the temporal plates used to create it, is a precious design tool starting from the idea that the future structure can be inserted organically within the historical series by assuming the sum of the transformations, and not just their visible result, as the starting point of the design action.

2_3 **CLASSIFYING RECONSTRUCTION**

Once the redrawing of case studies has been carried out, it is necessary to construct a classification system capable of confronting and evaluating the results of the different strategies adopted. However, the different time frames, conjunctural economic and social conditions, make any attempt at systematization extremely difficult. Marcello Mamoli and Giorgio Trebbi, in their work *L'Europa del Secondo Dopoguerra* (1988) within the seminal series *Storia dell'Urbanistica* published by Laterza, proposed a possible classification. Published in 1988, the book remains one of the most updated instances of comparative research in the field of urban design following conflicts. However, the categories individuated are purely storiographic and based on archival research and personal judgment; and most of the research work focuses on the planning rather than on the concrete results of urban metamorphosis. It is necessary to develop an alternative quantitative classification mechanism capable of confronting evolutions in the urban patterns and to identify the key parameters that constitute the working tools for the modification of the built environment.

Mamoli and Trebbi's subdivision is made up of four categories, imagined for World War II Europe but potentially applicable (with minor adjustments) to other effects resulting from extreme events:

a. ### AS IT WAS WHERE IT WAS

.

In cities that carefully maintained heritage and memory by reconstructing the same urban pattern with same building types (St. Malo, Münster, Warsaw, Florence, etc.).

b. ### CONTINUITY BETWEEN
TRADITION AND INNOVATION

.

An innovative compromise that while mandating the urban pattern inserts new building types within a vision of modernization and functional improvement (Amiens, Caen, Lübeck, Terni, Milan, etc.).

c. ### RUPTURE WITH THE PAST

.

A denunciation of destruction as an irreversible loss leading to a new urban pattern defined with new techniques yet with similar building types (Hannover, Frankfurt, Livorno, Coventry, etc.).

d. ### PROGRAMMATIC INNOVATION

.

In the few cases where reconstruction has been seen as a chance for true re-foundation with a completely new urban pattern and new building types (Le Havre, Rotterdam, etc.).

Despite the valuable effort, this classification fails to fully equip designers with clear evaluations of the results of each approach that can act as an engine for future reconstruction efforts facing current urban pressures.

In order to construct a qualitative tool for designers, we have developed a mathematical method for evaluating and comparing different cases based

2_ HISTORICAL EXPERIENCES

↑ Bochum / DEU 1943–1965

↑ Bremen / DEU 1944–2021

↑ Caen / FRA 1944–1957

↑ Cape Town, Joe Slovo Park / ZAF 2000–2021

↑ Corail Cesselesse / HAI 2010–2022

↑ Coventry / GBR 1943–1962

↑ Den Haag, Vogelwijk / NLD 1941–1965

↑ Detroit, Brush Park / USA 1943–2022

↑ Dresden / DEU 1945–2005

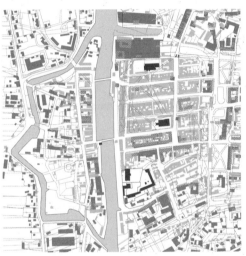

↑ Elblag / POL 1939–1983

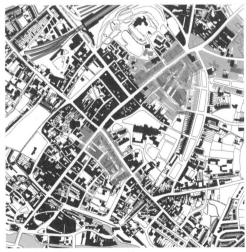

↑ Exeter / GBR 1942–1950

↑ Frankfurt am Main / DEU 1944–2010

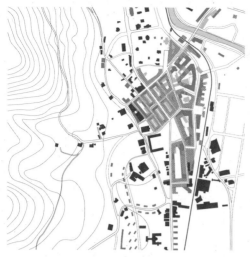

↑ Guernica / ESP 1937–1956

↑ Hamburg / DEU 1943–1960

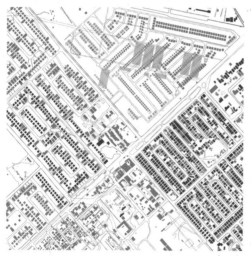

↑ Harare, Dzivarasekwa / ZBW 2008–2021

↑ Ho Chi Minh, District 8 / VTN 2003–2021

↑ Ifo, refugee camp Dadaab / KNY 2009–2021

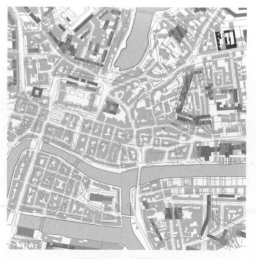

↑ Kaliningrad / RUS 1945–1998

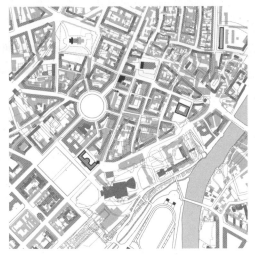

↑ Kassel / DEU 1943–1970

↑ Khuda Ki Basti / PAK 2007–2021

↑ Kobane / SYR 2014–2020

↑ Kutupalong / BAN 2009–2021

↑ Lagos, Makoko / NIG 2000–2021

↑ Le Havre / FRA 1944–1964

TRANSFORMATION
MAP

_____

HARARE DZIVARASEKWA

●

The neighborhood of
Dzivarasekwa in the western
part of Harare, the capital of
Zimbabwe, is the collateral
result of a government-initiated
slum clearance campaign that
started in 2005. Slum dwellers

of different parts of the city
were forcibly moved into
holding camps, including the
Dzivarasekwa Extension Camp.
In 2007, this camp, which initially
lacked any basic services, was
upgraded through a site and

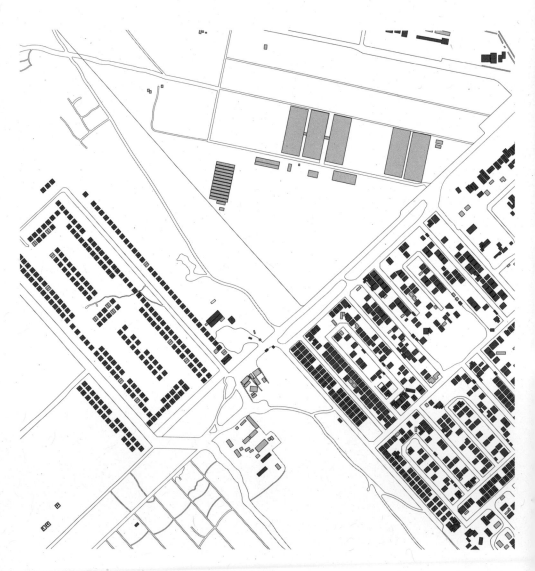

HARARE, DZIVARASEKWA / ZBW 2009

Destruction map. Destroyed and preserved buildings.

service approach, allocating to the residents plots of land and a bare minimum of essential infrastructure. Dzivarasekwa grew at an extraordinary pace, and in 2010 it was chosen as the pilot settlement for the citywide Harare Slum Upgrading Project (HSUP). The transformation map of the area shows the hybrid nature of the impetuous urban growth: the progressive saturation of the original site and service area, the upgrading of the first additions with new basic infrastructures, the complete substitution of selected parts, and the increasing measure of self-built, spontaneous urban patterns inserted into the preexisting grid.

HARARE, DZIVARASEKWA / ZBW 2021
Reconstruction map. Preserved and reconstructed buildings.

- _Preserved buildings
- _Destroyed buildings
- _Reconstructed buildings
- _Reconstruction on destruction

2_ HISTORICAL EXPERIENCES

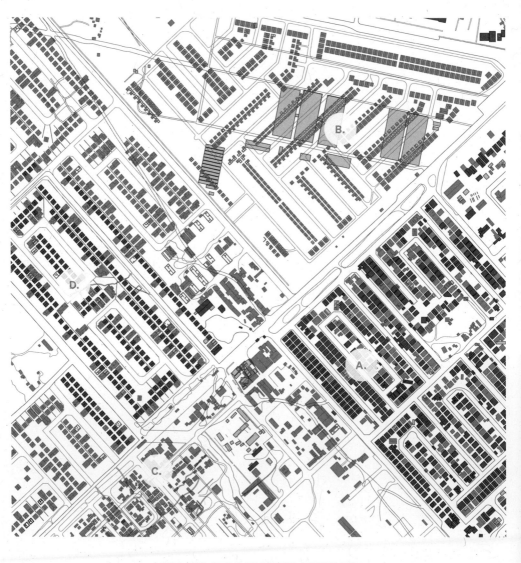

HARARE, DZIVARASEKWA / ZBW 2009–2021

Transformation map. Destroyed, preserved, and reconstructed buildings.

A. Filling. New buildings complete the existing allotment.
B. Replacement. New buildings form a new urban layout.
C. Urban growth. New buildings form a discontinuous expansion.
D. Upgrading. New buildings over existing buildings.

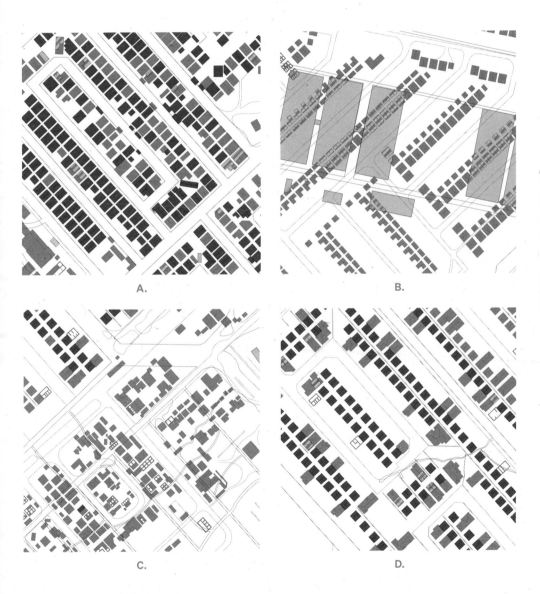

A.

B.

C.

D.

2_ HISTORICAL EXPERIENCES

↑ Lefkōsia/Lefkoşa / CYP 1921–2020

↑ Lima, Cerro Verde / PER 2005–2021

↑ Lima, Villa El Salvador / PER 2002–2020

↑ London, Barbican / GBR 1940–1982

↑ Lübeck / DEU 1942–1960

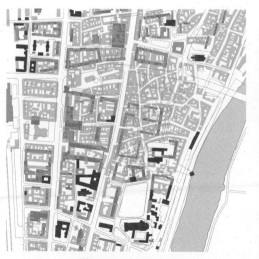

↑ Magdeburg / DEU 1945–1980

↑ Marseille, Vieux Port / FRA 1943–1958

↑ Middelburg / NLD 1940–1971

↑ Milano / ITA 1944–1965

↑ Al Muharraq / BHR 1950–2020

↑ München / DEU 1944–1983

↑ Münster / DEU 1944–1964

↑ Nahr el Bared / LEB 2003–2010

↑ Nairobi, Kibera / KNY 2002–2022

↑ New Orleans, Lower Ninth Ward / USA 2005–2020

↑ New York, South Bronx / USA 1952–2022

↑ Nürnberg / DEU 1945–1971

↑ Orléans, Bourgogne-République / FRA 1940–1960

↑ Pisa / ITA 1943–1960

↑ Plymouth / GBR 1940–1962

↑ Poznań / POL 1939–1965

↑ Rimini / ITA 1943–1965

↑ Rotterdam / NLD 1940–1955

↑ Saint Louis, De Soto Carr / USA 1952–1976

↑ Saint Malo / FRA 1944–1961

↑ Terni / ITA 1943–1954

↑ Tindouf, El Aaiun / ALG 2003–2022

↑ Torino / ITA 1943–1959

↑ Tours / FRA 1940–1962

↑ Tulsa, Greenwood / USA 1921–1962

↑ Valparaíso, Cerro Merced / CIL 2014–2021

↑ Venzone / ITA 1976–1991

↑ Warsaw, Muranow / POL 1939–1956

↑ Wien / AUT 1945–1963

↑ Wroclaw / POL 1939–1965

↑ Zaatari / JOR 2013–2021

on the careful analysis of transformation maps and on their processing through an algorithm created specifically for this task [BROWN ET AL. 2010]. We compiled a list of eighteen indicators related to pre-destruction and reconstruction of built-up area, number of urban elements, median size of elements, average distance, and percentage of built area. The statistical analysis of the indicators permits a selection of those most relevant in influencing urban metamorphosis, allowing one to eliminate indicators underrepresented in terms of significance. A weighting of all eighteen indicators shows that those related to map transformation are among the most relevant, with a cumulative weight of more than 63 percent. A synoptic chart with the two axes defined by an indexed version of the parameters related to urban patterns and building types allows one to precisely locate each case study within a unique quantitative framework. The results of such a process tend to form a strongly polarized cloud with a clear correlation between the degree of urban and architectural innovation. This result confirms the idea that choices in the urban model strongly influence levels of density, and act as a form factor of the architectural elements by inducing specific design choices. The use of quantitative parameters allows one to construct a basic understanding of prewar and postwar conditions freed from biases and acts as a fundamental base for the development of design strategies informed by data analysis and interpretation.

2.4   **UNPRECEDENTED SCALE OF DESTRUCTION**

Despite the desperate need for an organized knowledge of reconstruction processes, to be seen as a starting point in the development of a discipline of reconstruction, it is fundamental to admit that the current pressures imposed on urban environments are unprecedented in the history of humanity in terms of scale and intensity. In the field of urbicide, the biggest city completely obliterated during World War II was Warsaw with its 1.3 million inhabitants, while Dresden or Coventry, which remained in popular culture for the harshness of their carpet bombing, had only 650,000 and 260,000 residents; and Hiroshima, martyrized by the first atomic bomb, had around 345,000. Today, the complete destruction of metropolises such as Aleppo (4.6 million), Mosul (1.8 million), or Sanaa (3.5 million) and the attacks on Kyiv (2.3 million) pose new and distressing questions related to the scale of urban warfare, while military strategists are already discussing the possibilities of war in megacities [HARRIS ET AL. 2014; KONAEV 2019].

The most striking and fast increase in global risk arises through climate-related disasters, which are growing at a pace never experienced before: 83 percent, from 3,656 events during the 1980–99 period to 6,681 in the past twenty years [VAN LOENHOUT AND BELOW 2019]. Major floods have more than doubled, the number of severe storms has risen 40 percent, and there have been major increases in droughts, wildfires, and heat waves. Climate change will most likely completely alter entire territories at a geographical scale and force societally disruptive urban shifts. Indonesia will relocate its sinking capital Jakarta, and a large part of its 10 million inhabitants, to the new city of Nusantara, recently established on the island of Sumatra [LYONS 2019], while Egypt and South Korea are considering a similarly extreme solution. Climate induced rural-urban migration is seen as a concurring trigger for present-day violence in Syria, Libya, and Yemen [FEMIA AND WERRELL 2013; GLEICK 2014], while large parts of the Middle East / North Africa (MENA) region have been labeled as uninhabitable by 2050 [ZITTIS ET AL. 2021] and the foreseen climate migrants of the next fifteen years have been projected to reach the staggering number of 216 million [CLEMENT ET AL. 2021].

The climate crisis has often been seen as the great equalizer [PARSONS 2007], capable of uniting humanity toward the common goal of saving the Earth, but in reality the Gini coefficient defining the level of inequality is reaching its historical peak in practically every nation: "we are facing the same storm, but we are in different boats" [NAKATE 2022]. An unequal society is threatening not only for the poorest strata of the local and global population but also for the community at large: California, by far the richest state in the richest country on Earth, is experiencing a housing crisis and rising homeless population due to its enormous wealth gap [DOUGHERTY 2021], posing doubts about the chance of survival of a highly unsustainable model [MANJOO 2019]. Dubai, the ivory tower where it is possible to ski in the middle of the desert, has become the only truly global urban model and the home of "dubaization" [ELSHESHTAWY 2009], a synonym for grandiose urban interventions that hide disadvantaged migrant laborers in slave-like working conditions and an enormous waste of resources that is pushing the planet further and further toward its destruction [DAVIS 2006].

A key difference in the current cities subjected to major pressures is the type of urban pattern involved: until World War II and in the immediate postwar years, the vast majority of destruction following extreme events occurred in dense historical cores with buildings of significant heritage value. Today, on the contrary, 90 percent of destruction happens in postindustrial urban patterns with very low urban quality. This peculiar situation requires design strategies which, rather than simply restoring previous conditions, ameliorate in qualitative and quantitative terms the future cities and lead the sustainable transition. To be able to face such epochal challenges, it is fundamental to imagine and construct a new urban model, one capable of a radical modification of current urban forms. The scarce urban quality of postindustrial areas, of informal settlements lacking basic services, and of planned peripheries that obsessively re-propose a single architectural type requires additional effort in providing the local population not only with housing, electricity, water, and sanitation, but also with meaningful urban patterns: "perhaps the best definition of the city in its higher aspects is to say that it is a place designed to offer the widest facilities for significant conversation" [MUMFORD 1961].

QUALITATIVE AND QUANTITATIVE CLASSIFICATION

The qualitative classification of the case studies starts from the four categories proposed by Mamoli and Trebbi in 1988 (as it was, where it was, with continuity between tradition and innovation, a break with the past, programmatic innovation) to construct a synoptic chart that describes the permanence or modification of the building type (X axis) and of the urban pattern (Y axis). Each category occupies a quadrant, and each case study is positioned based on the interpretative analyses of available literature. The quantitative classification

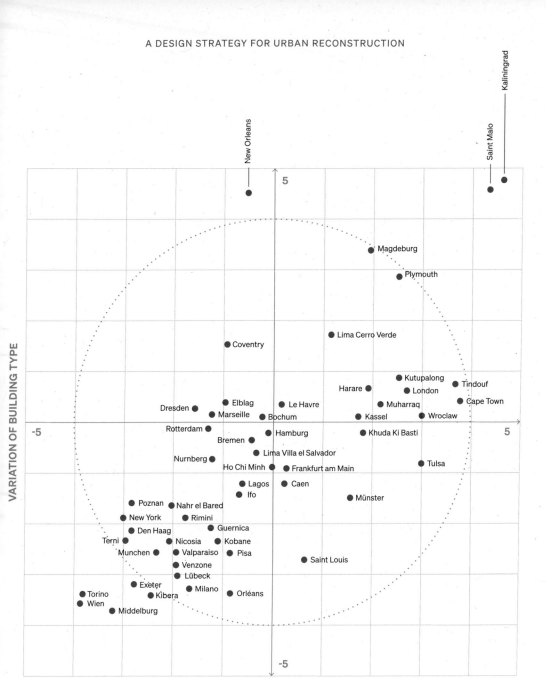

VARIATION OF BUILDING TYPE

VARIATION OF URBAN PATTERN

Kaliningrad

Saint Malo

New Orleans

5

Magdeburg

Plymouth

Lima Cerro Verde

Coventry

Kutupalong

Harare · London · Tindouf

Dresden · Elblag · Le Havre · Muharraq · Cape Town

Marseille · Bochum · Kassel · Wroclaw

-5 · Rotterdam · Hamburg · Khuda Ki Basti · 5

Bremen

Nurnberg · Lima Villa el Salvador

Ho Chi Minh · Frankfurt am Main · Tulsa

Lagos · Caen

Ifo

Poznan · Nahr el Bared · Münster

New York · Rimini

Den Haag · Guernica

Terni · Nicosia · Kobane

Munchen · Valparaiso · Pisa

Venzone · Saint Louis

Lübeck

Exeter · Milano

Torino · Kibera · Orléans

Wien

Middelburg

-5

is a mathematical analysis that confronts, for each case study, a series of indicators of urban metamorphosis derived from the transformation maps (percentage of land occupation, number of elements, median size, destroyed area, etc.). The analysis defines a building transformation score for each case study, allowing the construction of a synoptic chart where the position of each case study is given by the variation of its specific score from the average of all the cases.

3.

STRATEGY

Reconstruction needs a completely new design strategy, a subversion of current city-making mechanisms that allows one to reinstate the community, with its aspirations and needs, as the center of the process of controlling urban metamorphosis. Four dichotomies define the required innovations: top-down / bottom-up, aspiring to a change in conceptual and operative approach; cataclysmic credit / gradual credit, proposing different financial mechanisms; layers /cells, sketching a new urban form; and project / process, aiming at a radical rethinking of design systems. The laboratory of reconstruction, an on-site space capable of hosting dialogues and activities, provides the toolbox required for the initiation of a successful switch in operational practices.

STRATEGY

•

3_1   TOP DOWN / BOTTOM UP

It is impossible for the current design methods, forged by the masters of modernism in a completely different global scenario (TAFURI 1973; HEYNEN 1999), to intervene in complex urban and social environments and face the challenges posed by large-scale modifications of urban patterns. The rigidity of urban planning, architecture, and the construction sector is witnessed by their incapacity to provide solutions for reconstruction that go beyond shelter (CHARLESWORTH 2014), thus making it necessary to define a path toward an alternative urban vision. Current organizations, time frames, technologies, building techniques, construction companies, real-estate mechanisms, and design practices are all incapable of facing the uncertainty, conflict, and dissonance underlined by the urban metamorphoses triggered by the cities under pressure paradigm.

In the case of extreme events, the current approach, mainly applied by national state powers or transnational organizations, is a top-down vision that can be adapted with minor modifications to post-disaster "rebuilding" (SCHWAB 2014), informal settlement "upgrading" (BANERJEE ET AL. 2012; SKINNER ET AL. 2015), "build back better" mechanisms (UNITED NATIONS 2015), or "rehabilitation" of marginalized neighborhoods (BARTLING 2014). The top-down approach favors large companies that operate with sizable infrastructures and big financial loans. Urban metamorphosis is defined and undertaken as a single project that is run, often at a distance, by a large design firm, with coordination, execution, and timing problems. This top-down approach is completely detached from the needs and hopes of local communities and often leads to the establishment of infrastructures and services that are out of scale and unmanageable in the long term. Most importantly, the top-down approach fails to break the cycle of violence, poverty, and insecurity, and it is incapable of building peace and transitioning toward a sustainable future.

It is necessary to switch toward an opposite bottom-up strategy by defining new design tools that accept the necessary undefined nature of the final

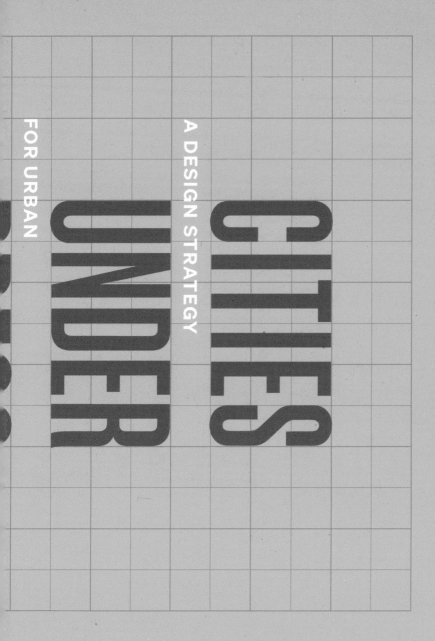

FOR URBAN

A DESIGN STRATEGY

CITIES

UNDER

T / JACOPO GALLI

CITIES UNDER PRESSURE

A DESIGN STRATEGY FOR URBAN RECONSTRUCTION

Dear Robert Bevan,

It is a great pleasure for me to send you the book Cities Under Pressure that I wrote with Benno Albrecht.

Your book, The Destruction of Memory was very useful in our

RESEARCH AND I WOULD LOVE
TO HEAR YOUR THOUGHTS ON THE
DESIGN STRATEGY WE DEVELOPED

BEST REGARDS

→ urbicidetaskforce@iuav.it

RECONSTRUCTION

PRESS
URE.

ARCHI
TANGLE

BENNO ALBRECH

results within a guiding urban vision (SENNETT 1970; SENDRA AND SENNETT 2020). A bottom-up approach imagines design processes as something to be ideated and conducted directly with and by the local community, through the self-organization of a local workforce. We have to start from the assumption that the reconstructed city of the future might (and often should) be completely different in character from the current city that has hosted and favored violence, social distress, or disaster. The bottom-up approach applies not only to urban patterns and territories, but also to cultural and social systems, as well as to economic structures and administrative organizations. The alternative approach leads to a complete rethinking of design disciplines by imagining urban design as a regeneration tool that triggers continuous, complex, creative, unforeseeable, circular, and sustainable changes.

3_2   CATACLYSMIC CREDIT / GRADUAL CREDIT

A bottom-up strategy starts with small loans given to many people and implies a city generated by a sum of small interventions that together shape the urban environment and are continuously negotiated with a centralized power, the role of which should be limited to the few choices that cannot be made at the lower level. Currently, extreme events generate high media attention and external financial support that tends to rapidly fade away in the medium- or long-term time frame once media coverage has been attracted to different areas. Donors and international support flow conspicuously in the immediate aftermath of a destructive event, but the lack of a general strategy often leads to the construction of "white elephants" (ROBINSON AND TORVIK 2005; BOWEN 2009) which, rather than initiate positive economic and social cycles, are investment projects with a negative social surplus.

A top-down approach focused on big-size intervention tends to minimize the local content (OLAWUYI 2021) of reconstruction operations, often leaving only around 10–15 percent of the total financial budget on site, while the greatest amount of funding is drained by big international firms, the only ones able to participate in large-scale reconstruction operations. The current approach is incapable of generating a "lanes' economy" (GRIMA ET AL. 2020), where the benefit of reconstruction funding trickles down to the local community or even guarantees local employment, the only possible tool to sustain urban reconstruction in the long run.

Cities and territories involved in extreme events remain under the lens of the global public opinion for a short period and are then "helped" by an external hand that provides immediate relief, but in the longer term deprives the local community of the economic support and social strength necessary for a durable reconstruction. In the 1960s, Jane Jacobs had already pointed out the importance of

3 _ STRATEGY

TOP DOWN

●

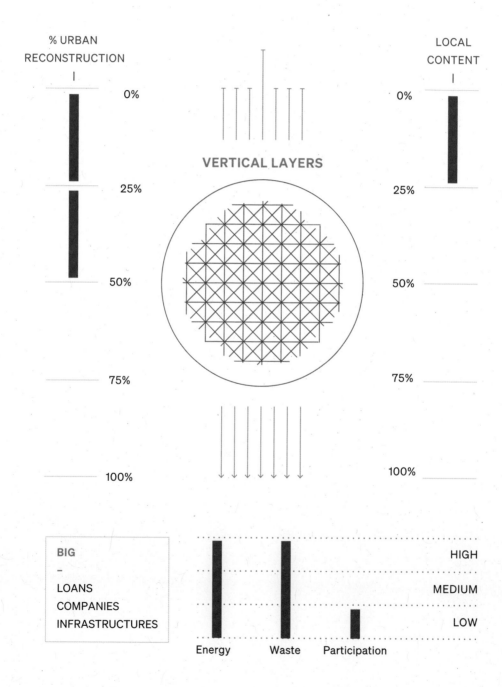

% URBAN
RECONSTRUCTION

|

0%

25%

50%

75%

100%

LOCAL
CONTENT

|

0%

25%

50%

75%

100%

VERTICAL LAYERS

BIG
–
LOANS
COMPANIES
INFRASTRUCTURES

HIGH

MEDIUM

LOW

Energy   Waste   Participation

BOTTOM UP

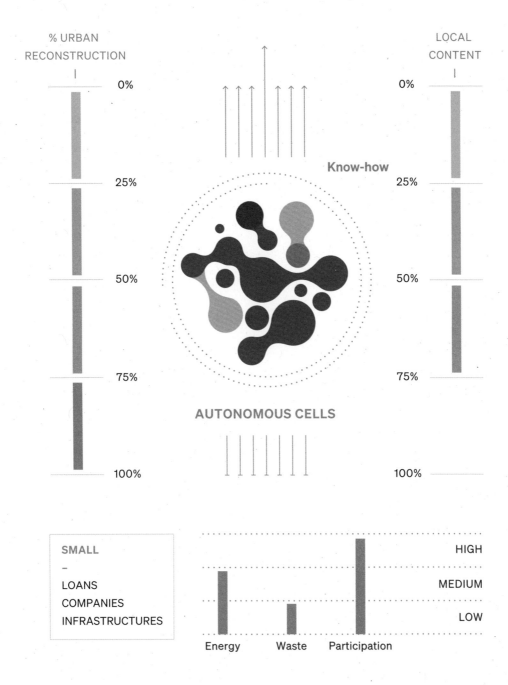

% URBAN
RECONSTRUCTION

0%

25%

50%

75%

100%

Know-how

AUTONOMOUS CELLS

LOCAL
CONTENT

0%

25%

50%

75%

100%

SMALL

–

LOANS
COMPANIES
INFRASTRUCTURES

HIGH

MEDIUM

LOW

Energy   Waste   Participation

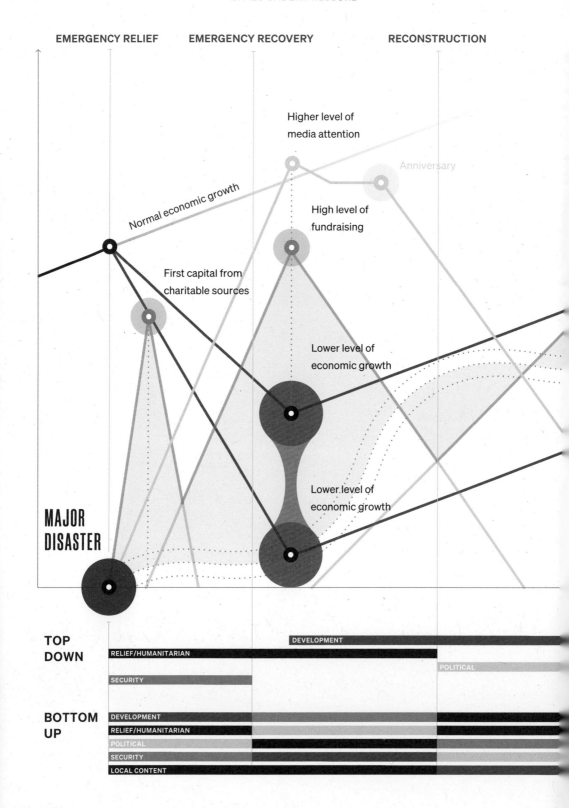

EMERGENCY RELIEF   EMERGENCY RECOVERY   RECONSTRUCTION

Higher level of
media attention

Anniversary

Normal economic growth

High level of
fundraising

First capital from
charitable sources

Lower level of
economic growth

Lower level of
economic growth

MAJOR
DISASTER

TOP
DOWN

DEVELOPMENT

RELIEF/HUMANITARIAN

POLITICAL

SECURITY

BOTTOM
UP

DEVELOPMENT

RELIEF/HUMANITARIAN

POLITICAL

SECURITY

LOCAL CONTENT

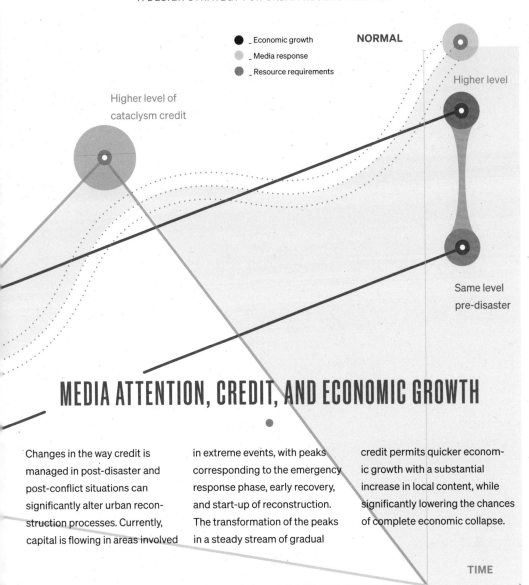

_ Economic growth
_ Media response
_ Resource requirements

NORMAL

Higher level

Higher level of
cataclysm credit

Same level
pre-disaster

MEDIA ATTENTION, CREDIT, AND ECONOMIC GROWTH

Changes in the way credit is managed in post-disaster and post-conflict situations can significantly alter urban reconstruction processes. Currently, capital is flowing in areas involved in extreme events, with peaks corresponding to the emergency response phase, early recovery, and start-up of reconstruction. The transformation of the peaks in a steady stream of gradual credit permits quicker economic growth with a substantial increase in local content, while significantly lowering the chances of complete economic collapse.

TIME

credit as the cornerstone for triggering positive urban metamorphosis, in her book *The Death and Life of Great American Cities*: "money shapes cataclysmic changes in cities. Relatively little of it shapes gradual change. Cataclysmic money pours into an area in concentrated form, producing drastic changes. . . . three kinds of money behave not like irrigation systems, bringing life-giving streams to feed steady, continual growth. Instead, they behave like manifestations of malevolent climates beyond the control of man—affording either searing droughts or torrential, eroding floods. . . . City building that has a solid footing produces continual and gradual change, building complex diversifications" (JACOBS 1961).

A qualitative reconstruction must start from the modification of a credit system that, rather than acting as a cataclysmic force on the city, must become a gradual chance for continuous, positive modification. Financial support can be split into a myriad of smaller loans, provided that a guiding principle of design and a control mechanism have been put in place. Smaller loans given to local workers have a much greater chance of remaining in the local economic flow and generate further benefits on site. Gradual credit can be distributed, with forms of solidarity lending (ARMENDÁRIZ AND MORDUCH 2005; YUNUS 2007) applied to groups of community members willing to reconstruct their home or business and also to small-scale entrepreneurs who can produce materials or provide services required in the reconstruction process. The bottom-up approach must be matched with a radically different financial model that entails different goals: from the quicker possible return to a stable condition to the management of a fluid one in which the urban pattern undergoes continuous modification, permitted and favored by a new distribution of credit.

3_3   **LAYERS / CELLS**

The top-down approach that characterizes current city-making processes is carried out in the urban environment through the development and application of a series of layers: infrastructures (MARX 2022), water distribution (BAKER 2009), energy supply (EICKER 2018), public and private housing (ROLNIK 2019), or basic services (JUNGINGER 2016). Each layer is seen as a detached subject with its specific professional figures, construction mechanisms, and service providers. Often, key design decisions affecting urban forms are not planned in light of the desired urban features but as responses to a sum of input linked to one or more layers; the final result is a dull urban environment that is capital-centric, speculation-driven, and investment-dominated, that is incapable of achieving sustainability in an integrated vision, and, more importantly, that is lacking any kind of urban quality given by significant mixed-use spaces.

The layered vision of the city leads inevitably to low-density and low-quality urban sprawl [BRUEGMAN 2005], a monofunctional city that, while representing on average 90 percent of urban environments, is the symptom of a development model which wastes natural resources, minimizes social interaction, and forces an outdated lifestyle [BROWN 2009; KEUCHEYAN 2014]. Despite relevant cultural and economic differences, global urban sprawl tends to show homogenization and hypersimplification processes. Rather than be built to host lively communities, it seems to be constructed "for privatized consumption built around the car and celebrated at the mall; for residential enclaves that exclude those deemed undesirable; for the security of gated communities and fortified leisure centers; and for a predictable homogeneity of built forms that imply safe investments" [HARRIS 2015].

Emergency response systems in the case of extreme events accelerate the production of sprawled urban patterns: the top-down approach applied through a vertical order—subdivided into functions (infrastructures, education, health, etc.) and entrusted to different organizations (local administration, international organizations, NGOs, etc.)—generates urban spaces with the sole objective of sheltering the highest possible number of people in the shortest possible time. It is a noble goal, which, however, does not produce a true urban environment but rather a soulless repetition of living modules, regardless of their technological and constructive quality.

The alternative is a city imagined as an organic constellation of cells, a recurring idea that submerges and resurfaces continuously in the history of urban design [PIACENTI 2022]. Urban destruction can be the chance to completely reverse current settlement mechanisms in favor of a city formed by a sum of defined and self-contained urban cells, autonomous elements of a calibrated dimension [MUMFORD 1961] that can dialogue with each other and host a population of around 10,000 inhabitants each with a high constructive density. Urban cells can be defined and built through a series of delocalized, small, and widespread interventions that allow one to act simultaneously in multiple different areas, optimizing time, financial resources, infrastructure, and workforce while minimizing land consumption and waste. The reconstruction of large-scale urban settlements can be achieved as a sum of small cells, connected with low-impact sustainable infrastructure and subdivided by green-productive areas. The defined scale of the cells allows local communities at the neighborhood scale to become the protagonists of reconstruction through communitarian design mechanisms and direct intervention [LOZANO 1990].

The urban cell model strengthens community bonds, and it can even act as a seed for peace in violent situations, while the small scale of the interventions permits intervention in fluid conditions, stabilizes small areas, defines short- and long-term goals, and strengthens resilience and attachment to place.

3_ STRATEGY

HISTORICAL CORES AND URBAN SPRAWL

●

In order to comprehend the average size of historical cores in relationship to the overall dimension of cities, we carried out a redrawing of twenty case studies in the European and Middle Eastern regions (Aleppo, Amsterdam, Barcelona, Berlin, Beirut, Cairo, Damascus, Jerusalem, Lisboa, London, Madrid, Marrakech, Milano, Mosul, Paris, Sanaa, Stockholm, Tripoli, Tunis, Wien). The cities are represented using three different colors: one for the historical core and older parts of the city with high density (average of 2.7 sqm/sqm); the second for the first extensions, carried out in the twenty-first century or early twentieth century at a medium density level (approx. 1.5 sqm/sqm); and the third for urban sprawl, built in the second part of the twentieth century at low density (0.3–1.0 sqm/sqm). Calculations made on the basis of the redrawing allow one to identify that historical cores, on average, represent 1–4 percent of the total city, first extensions 3–6 percent, while the vast majority of the city, over 90 percent, is urban sprawl.

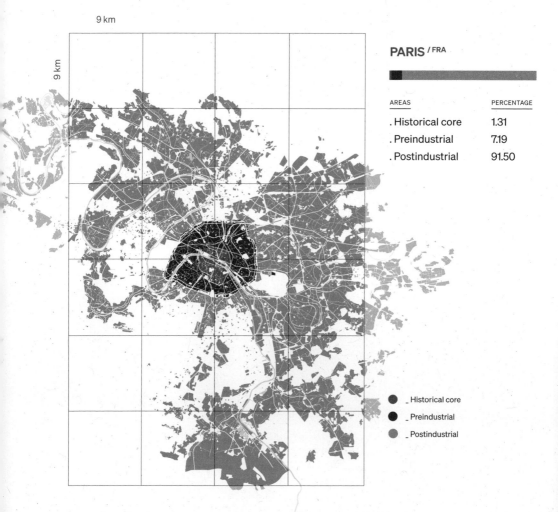

9 km

9 km

PARIS / FRA

AREAS	PERCENTAGE
. Historical core	1.31
. Preindustrial	7.19
. Postindustrial	91.50

● _ Historical core
● _ Preindustrial
● _ Postindustrial

AMSTERDAM / NLD

AREAS	PERCENTAGE
. Historical core	3.76
. Preindustrial	23.30
. Postindustrial	72.94

CAIRO / EGY

AREAS	PERCENTAGE
. Historical core	3.48
. Preindustrial	5.95
. Postindustrial	90.57

WIEN / AUT

AREAS	PERCENTAGE
. Historical core	0.75
. Preindustrial	5.99
. Postindustrial	93.26

9 km

9 km

BARCELONA / ESP

AREAS	PERCENTAGE
. Historical core	2.09
. Preindustrial	4.69
. Postindustrial	93.22

9 km

9 km

● _ Historical core
● _ Preindustrial
● _ Postindustrial

9 km

9 km

BEIRUT / LBN

AREAS	PERCENTAGE
. Historical core	1.12
. Preindustrial	4.48
. Postindustrial	94.40

9 km

9 km

MADRID / ESP

AREAS	PERCENTAGE
. Historical core	1.19
. Preindustrial	2.99
. Postindustrial	95.82

9 km

9 km

LISBOA / PRT

AREAS	PERCENTAGE
. Historical core	6.56
. Preindustrial	20.32
. Postindustrial	73.12

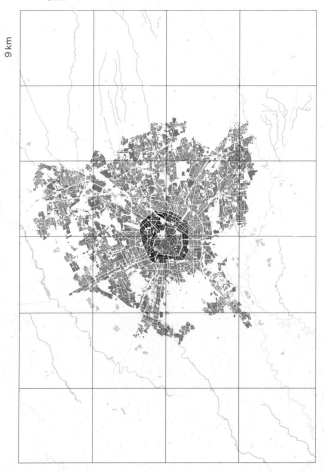

9 km

9 km

MILANO / ITA

AREAS	PERCENTAGE
. Historical core	2.65
. Preindustrial	6.05
. Postindustrial	91.30

● _ Historical core
● _ Preindustrial
● _ Postindustrial

9 km

9 km

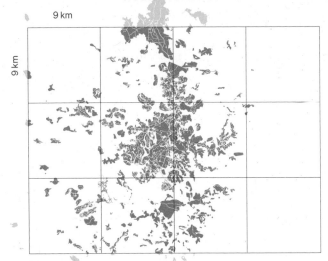

JERUSALEM / ISR

AREAS	PERCENTAGE
. Historical core	0.43
. Preindustrial	0
. Postindustrial	99.57

9 km

9 km

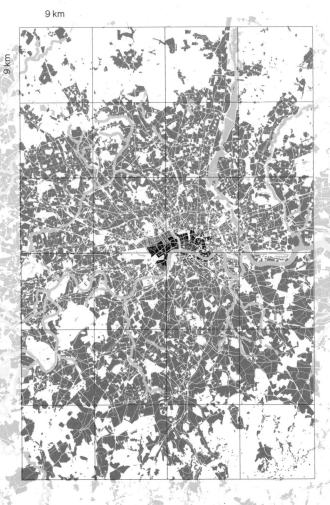

LONDON / GBR

AREAS	PERCENTAGE
. Historical core	0.22
. Preindustrial	0.79
. Postindustrial	98.99

HISTORICAL CORES AND URBAN SPRAWL UNDER PRESSURE

●

The maps overlap the type of urban pattern with the destruction of buildings, showing how urban sprawl makes up the vast majority of urban area affected by extreme events.

The diverse urban patterns react in different ways to pressure: historical cores are fragile in terms of materials, but the slow process of trial and error that allowed their current definition guarantees high resilience. On the contrary, urban sprawl is often not able to quickly adapt to shocks, and its monofunctionality can dirctly escalate the crisis to affect the whole urban environment.

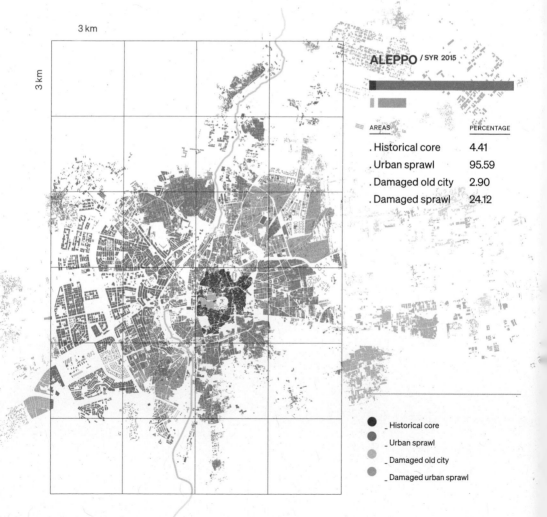

3 km

3 km

ALEPPO / SYR 2015

AREAS	PERCENTAGE
. Historical core	4.41
. Urban sprawl	95.59
. Damaged old city	2.90
. Damaged sprawl	24.12

● _ Historical core
● _ Urban sprawl
● _ Damaged old city
● _ Damaged urban sprawl

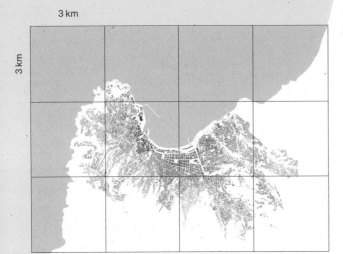

3 km

3 km

VALPARAISO / CHL 2014

AREAS	PERCENTAGE
. Historical core	2.40
. Urban sprawl	97.60
. Damaged old city	0
. Damaged sprawl	2.60

3 km

3 km

MARIUPOL / UKR 2022

AREAS	PERCENTAGE
. Historical core	2.87
. Urban sprawl	97.13
. Damaged old city	2.53
. Damaged sprawl	40.16

3 km

FROM SPRAWL
TO CELLS

●

The process of metamorphosis of the urban form, from the current low-density urban sprawl to the future urban cells, can paradoxically be favored by the large-scale destruction that characterizes cities under pressure. Extreme events provide an extraordinary chance to radically rethink urban models, starting from the idea that the reconstructed city of the future can be, and often should be, different in terms of space and features from the pre-event conditions. The scarce quantitative performance and qualitative features of current urban sprawl must be substituted by a new urban pattern capable of increasing community well-being and resilience against future extreme events.

MOSUL / IRQ 2017

AREAS	PERCENTAGE
. Historical core	4.35
. Urban sprawl	95.65
. Damaged old city	3.33
. Damaged sprawl	11.87

_ Historical core
_ Urban sprawl
_ Damaged old city
_ Damaged urban sprawl

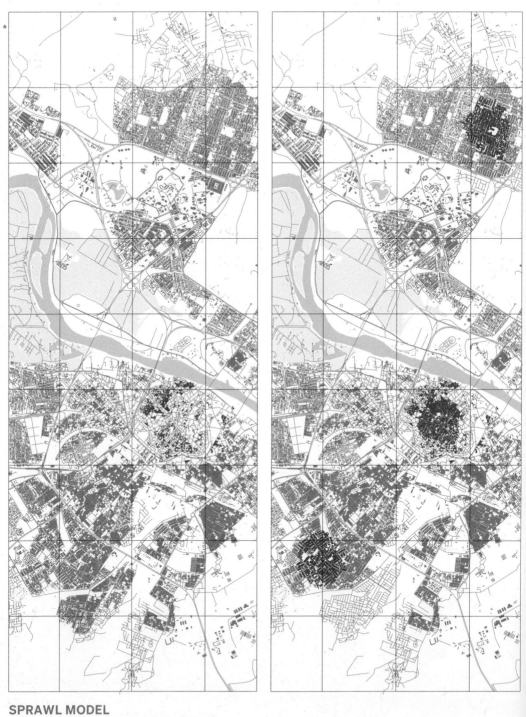

SPRAWL MODEL

Land occupation / green areas PERCENTAGE

69.35	5.9	24.68

60.61	14.71	24.68

Population density

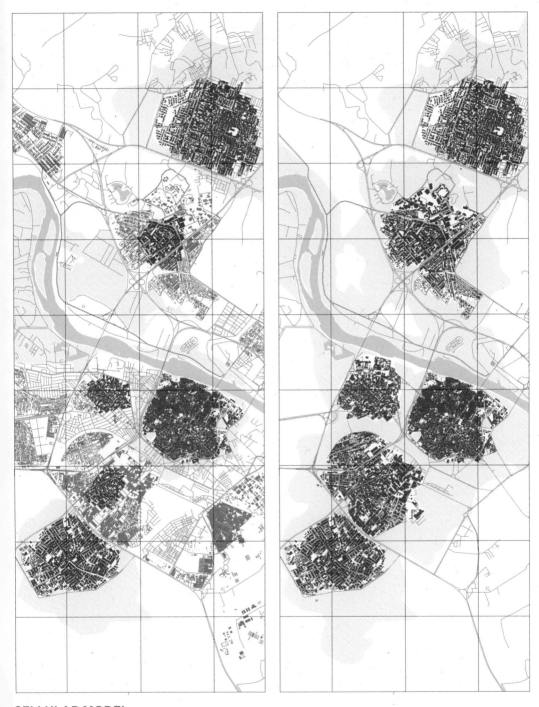

CELLULAR MODEL

Land occupation / green areas PERCENTAGE

| 19.26 | 29.13 | 51.61 | | 31.72 | 68.28 |

FROM SPRAWL TO CELLS

●

The formation of the urban cells is a process to be triggered, accompanied, and controlled, a goal that can be reached only in a medium to long time frame. Each cell operates in a bottom-up vision that benefits from direct intervention by the local community, permitting a maximization of diversity and innovation. The centralized level does not completely disappear but changes in scope and function; it operates as a mediator and facilitator between the different cells, favoring productive dialogues and exchanges, while defining and constructing the connective tissue of the city with key issues such as infrastructures and green areas.

MOSUL / **IRQ FUTURE**

■▨▨▨▨▨▨▨▨▨▨▨▨▨▨▨▨▨

AREAS	PERCENTAGE
. New cells	26.17
. Green areas	73.83

3 km

3 km

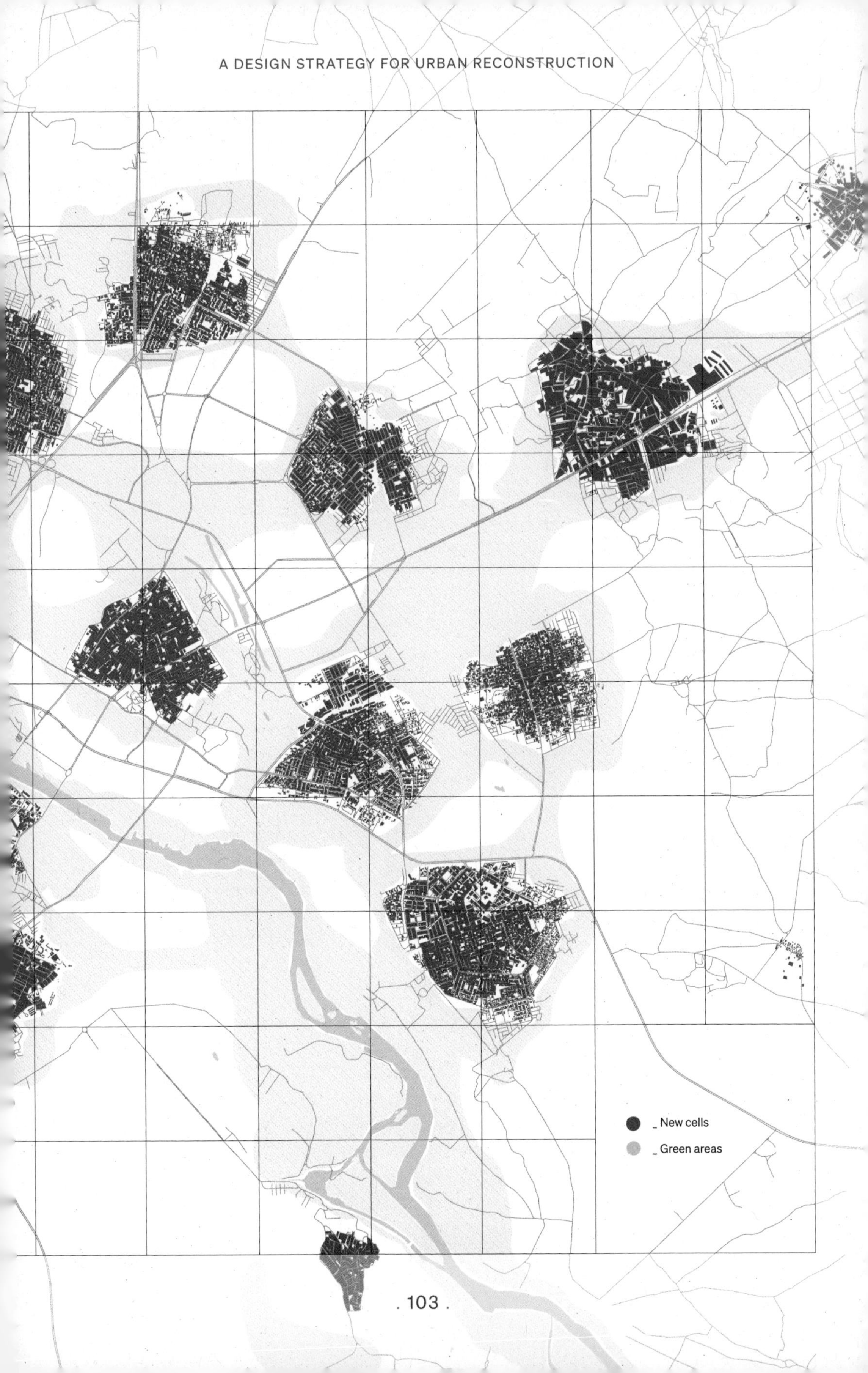

_ New cells

_ Green areas

3_4 PROJECT / PROCESS

The bottom-up approach, which can be triggered by a gradual credit distribution mechanism and define an urban cell settlement model, requires a completely innovative design approach capable of controlling rapid urban transformation. It is a design approach that moves away from the certainty of fixed projects to instead embrace the uncertainty and dissonance entailed by a process of progressive definition of the urban form in space and in time. The processual approach starts from the comprehension and acceptance of the impossibility of outlining a fixed design solution and rather embraces the role of the designer as a definer of settlement principles [GREGOTTI 1966] and controller of urban metamorphosis [ALBRECHT AND BENEVOLO 1990; BENEVOLO 1996] within a range of infinite variations. The designer becomes the shaper and controller of a set of parameters able to define the ever-changing borders of the possible modifications of the urban form.

The processual approach sees not only space but most importantly time as a central factor in the design mechanism. Time becomes a design factor, and the definition of the different phases contributes to the progressive shaping of spaces accounting for direct interventions and for the fluid responses to them. Rather than working through layers, design operates through phases where all of the different elements are present at various intensities, and the evolution of each element is inserted into a common logical framework, aiming not at the definition of a fixed condition but rather at the continuous renegotiation of a fluid and dynamic equilibrium [SALE 1985]. It is fundamental to abandon rigid tools, such as the master plan, the manifesto of the demiurge architect of modernity, to instead embrace the evolutive nature of the city in a vision that aims to create urban environments capable of ensuring safety, personal well-being, good health, and fruitful communitarian relationships. Urban design can be rediscovered as the control mechanism of the dynamic equilibrium: outlining a blurred scenario of the reconstruction process, foreseeing the possible tactics that allow one to reach an approximation of such a model, and defining malleable technical and conceptual tools that enable the initial vision to be achieved.

One notion emerges as central: the designer needs to abandon the search for a final stable solution in favor of the continuous exploration of a set of futures, all possible but none necessary. The design process becomes a practical manifestation of a *pensiero debole* [weak thought] [VATTIMO AND ROVATTI 1983] and attempts a definition of the slippery borders of a *progetto debole* [weak design] [NICOLIN 1989] or *progetto minore* [minor design] as defined by Camillo Boano: "a project idea that is able to scratch reality, engrave it and overcome it, but also to outline the best possible form of the world. One that also allows a constant redesign of its transformations, which strenuously resists by opposing its reduction and normalization" [BOANO 2020]. It is a sensitive design approach that embraces humbleness and aims to act as a seismographer of reality, accepts the impossibility of defining urban forms as absolute truths, and rediscovers the continuous states of disorder of urban environments as the main work material.

3_5 RECONSTRUCTION LABORATORY

It is almost impossible for current professionals to operate in a processual vision, for the relationship with power structures and administrative bureaucracies binds present-day organizations in the architecture and urban planning professions to top-down mechanisms. In order to operate with a different vision, it is necessary to define pragmatic and flexible operational systems [WORLD BANK 2020] so as to be able to account for rapid and unexpected changes. Reconstruction can be initiated through the establishment of an on-site laboratory, an organization capable of identifying drivers and enablers of sustainable peace and prosperity; the laboratory must be centered around communities and their livelihoods, around their access to services and their exercise of rights and opportunities, within a notion of community security that includes physical, personal, social, economic, and political security [ADLER AND BARNETT 1998].

Reconstruction laboratory is an evolution, and a substantial adaptation to contemporary technological and social innovation, to the "progressive development approach" policies [PAPPALARDO 2021] that have been defined, but scarcely applied, by international organizations as a response to the global housing crisis. There is a broad range of examples of alternative operational mechanisms for urban design: "Aided self-help" in Puerto Rico in the 1940s [CRANE 1944]; the "roof loan scheme" and "core housing" mechanisms in Ghana, the Philippines, and Singapore in the 1950s [ABRAMS AND KOENIGSBERGER 1956, 1959, 1963]; the "builder's yard approach" in Mexicali [ALEXANDER 1985]; "open work mechanisms" in PREVI Lima [TURNER 1976]; "interim urbanization" in Dandora [CAMINOS 1973]; the "district laboratory" in Otranto [DINI 1984] in the 1970s; "site and service" in Aranya, India [DOSHI 2019]; the "incremental development scheme" in Khuda-ki-Basti [ISMAIL 2002]; "slum upgrading" in the Favela-Bairro program in Brazil [MACHADO 2003]; and "open building supports" in the Netherlands [HABRAKEN 1999] in the 1990s.

The reconstruction laboratory is an organization (and perhaps a physical structure) that acts as a collector of ideas and a coordinator of intervention with one simple but extremely complex goal: the reconstruction of an urban environment matching high quantitative performance to a high quality of life for the community and its members. The laboratory can host multidisciplinary dialogues and local community participation, test small-scale components, recycled materials, and prototypes, initiate reconciliation activities while understanding needs and expectations, negotiate with the different administrative levels, teach the skills needed and

3_STRATEGY

AUTONOMOUS CELLS BOTTOM-UP STRATEGY / ADVANTAGES

3_ STRATEGY

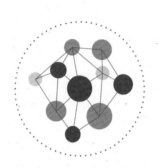

COORDINATION
—

The process involves citizens, institutions, productive chains, and communities in the design process, thus reducing blind spots.

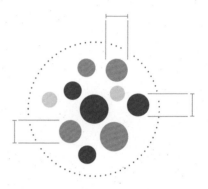

CONTROL
—

The cellular features of the strategy allow for immediate measurability and adaptability in terms of materials, techniques, typologies, etc.

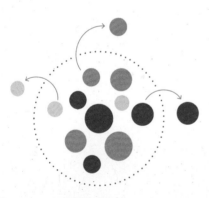

EMULATION
—

The design solutions are immediately replicable in other cells and neighborhoods, learning from mistakes and enhancing positive choices.

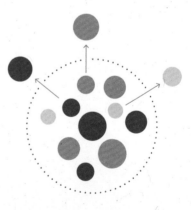

SCALABILITY
—

The strategy is applicable at different scales (building, cell, city, territory) through the application of the same concepts and operative tools.

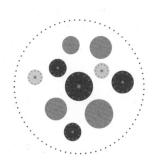

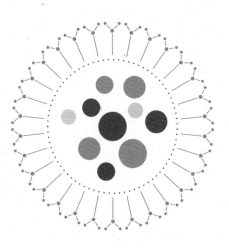

SECURE TIME FRAME

—

The strategy allows one to assess
time frames by considering multiple
variables and by setting goals for
short, medium, and long periods.

INVOLVEMENT

—

The local communities can participate
actively in self-produced reconstruction, activating a laboratory
of reconstruction for the triggering
and control of design processes.

3 _ STRATEGY

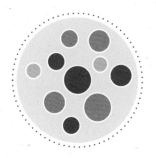

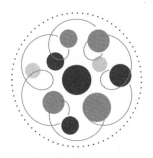

PLACE ATTACHMENT

—

The emotional bond between person
and place can be an engine for local
reconstruction, ensuring the
reestablishment of material and
immaterial heritage.

COMMUNITY DESIGN

—

A collaborative process allows one
to react to internal and external
changes and to quickly discharge
fixed schemes and recurring errors.

promote innovative research, define positive economic cycles and favor redistribution, give voice to marginalized groups, et cetera. The aim is not the substitution of design experts with amateur self-organized groups, but rather the construction of a new perspective that allows designers to understand their role within a complex process and to continuously reorient their actions in light of a series of interactions. The reconstruction laboratory moves away from any authorial claim to architecture and assumes the task of the continuous care of urban metamorphosis, steering it toward a dynamic equilibrium [BLEWITT 2018].

Possible disciplines interacting within the reconstruction laboratory include but are not limited to: agriculture, anthropology, art, automation, civil engineering, construction technology, cultural heritage, data science, demography, ecology, economics, energy, environmental studies, finance, food production, fundraising, health, history, law, management, materials, political science, pollution and waste, psychology, real estate, restoration, social science, sociology, statistics, structural engineering, sustainability, telecommunications, topography, transportation, tourism, water, and sanitation. The architect's role becomes that of collector and interpreter of infinite input, greatly enhancing the importance of its unicity as the only expert capable of immediately transforming concepts into living spaces.

3_6 **OPERATIONAL PHASES**

Post-disaster experts have proposed various subdivisions into phases of the complex emergency process following extreme events [UNDRR 1994, 2015, 2019; UNITED NATIONS 2008; EPA 2018]. This can be roughly summarized in a circular process consisting of four phases: mitigation, action taken to prevent or reduce the cause, impact, and consequences of disasters; preparedness, planning, training, and educational activities for events that cannot be mitigated; response, operations conducted in the immediate aftermath of a disaster to quickly ensure safety and well-being; and recovery, restoration, efforts that ensure a return to a stable condition [FEMA 2020]. The four phases are seen as segments of a cycle where the return period of each event dictates the general time frame that is then subdivided into significantly different intervals ranging from the continuous work of mitigation to the shortest possible duration of immediate response. In the current paradigm of emergency response, urban designers participate in all the phases but are more involved in the mitigation and recovery actions. In mitigation, they are called to anticipate and ensure the resilience of the built environment in the face of multiple pressures, while in recovery they are required to provide spatial solutions able to restore the state of dynamic equilibrium. Post-disaster frameworks can be partially adapted to conflicts and social and economic risks, but some differences emerge in the capacity of the local communities to actively participate in the process:

while natural disasters tend to strengthen community bonds (ALDRICH 2011; IRENI-SABAN 2012), wars act in exactly the opposite way by fracturing societies and generating dangerous grievances that can lead to conflict recurrence (VAUGHN 2011).

The proposed strategy partially challenges this division into phases by defining a system that, rather than working in a cycle, tends toward a linear modification of the built environment aiming at the definition of urban spaces that are different from the ones that have witnessed, and often favored, the impact of the extreme event. The Build Back Better paradigm defined as "the use of the recovery, rehabilitation and reconstruction phases after a disaster to increase the resilience of nations and communities through integrating disaster risk reduction measures into the restoration of physical infrastructure and societal systems, and into the revitalization of livelihoods, economies, and the environment" (UNGA 2016) must be criticized in terms of urban vision since it denies any chance for a radical modification of the urban environment. The critical issue of modifying the profound settlement principles of urban patterns, in order to make them resilient to major pressures, cannot be achieved by a strategy that is deliberately aimed at the restoration and amelioration of a pre-event condition.

The bottom-up cellular strategy, applied through laboratories of reconstruction, is instead aimed at the definition of a new urban pattern that analyses and considers the existing conditions, but at the same time is not blind to their a-critical repetition. In this vision, reconstruction does not necessarily imply a restoration of the existing urban form, which is often lacking urban qualities and technological performance, but only the search for a dynamic equilibrium capable of providing local communities with safe and qualitative urban spaces. The strategy reaffirms the necessity for preparedness and response but sees mitigation and recovery as a single element directed at the modification of the urban form and varying only in terms of intensity. Once the alternative urban model has been defined and its features understood, mitigation becomes a slow process of transformation, while recovery—or, for a better definition, reconstruction—is only to be intended as the extraordinary chance, applied in extreme situations, to significantly increase the speed of intervention and the pace of metamorphosis.

3_STRATEGY

PHASES OF EMERGENCY

●

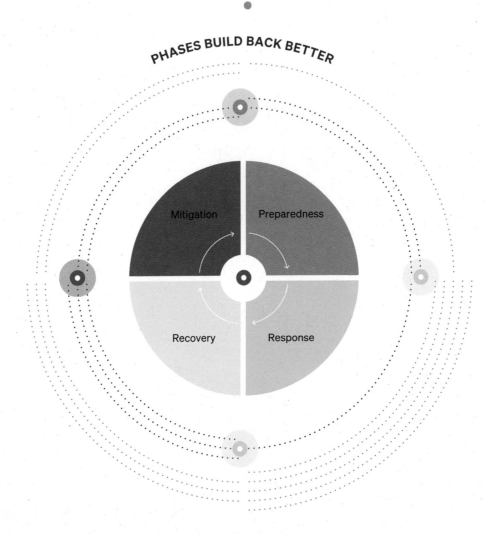

PHASES BUILD BACK BETTER

Mitigation

Preparedness

Recovery

Response

The scheme shows the necessary switch from current emergency intervention systems following extreme events to future approaches in the cities under pressure paradigm; the red cycle identifies the involvement of design experts and the orange cycle the required financial support. Current mechanisms operate with a build-back-better approach, constructing a cycle aimed at the reestablishment of pre-disaster conditions. The cities under pressure strategy starts from the assumption that the reconstructed city might vary significantly from the destroyed city and alters time frames, expert involvement, and financing systems accordingly.

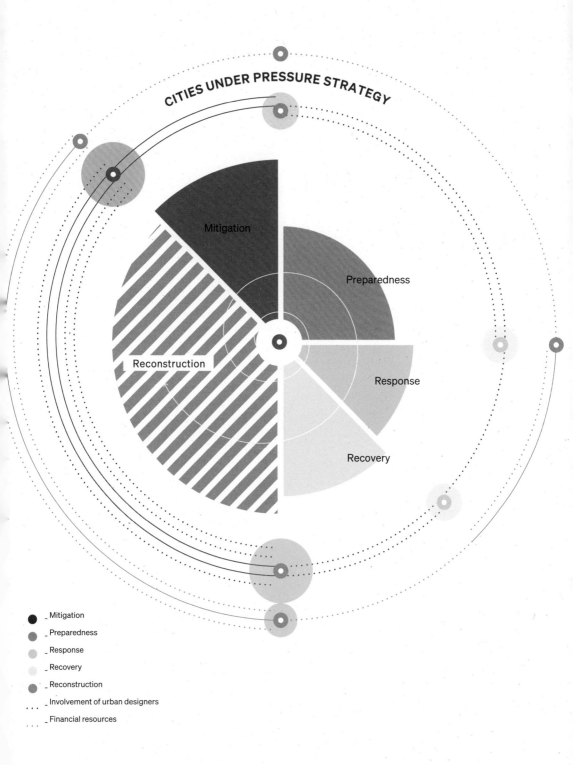

CITIES UNDER PRESSURE STRATEGY

Mitigation

Preparedness

Reconstruction

Response

Recovery

_ Mitigation
_ Preparedness
_ Response
_ Recovery
_ Reconstruction
_ Involvement of urban designers
_ Financial resources

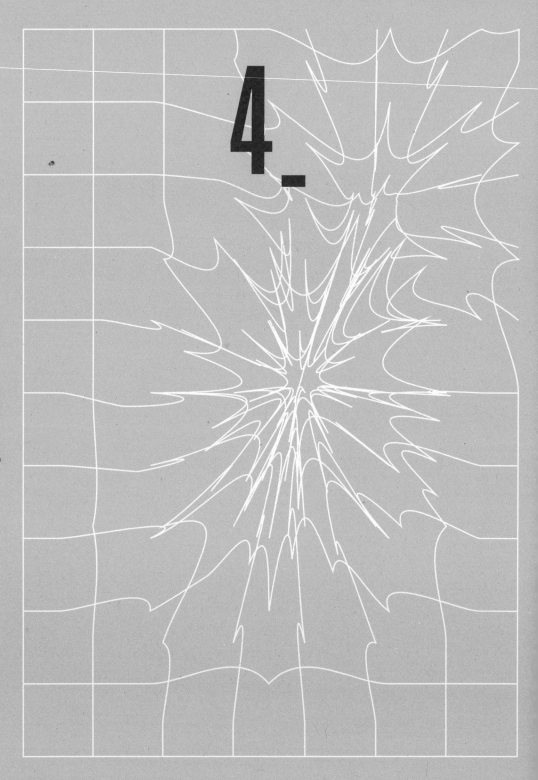

4.

SUSTAINABLE TRANSITION

The search for a societal model capable of preserving the Earth and guaranteeing a high quality of life for the generations to come is the biggest challenge currently faced by humanity. Urban design can actively participate in the transition process by employing innovative technologies and materials, allowing a major leap forward, but first and foremost through the complete rethinking of its models and practices. Historical cores are not simply testimonies to the possibility of a development system respectful of human and natural resources; they can also become operational models for the exportation of their qualitative and quantitative character to entire urban environments. The very existence of historical patterns testifies to the fact that adaptive circularity processes were possible in the past and are still possible today.

SUSTAINABLE TRANSITION

•

4_1 **EXPORTING THE HISTORICAL CORE**

Applying the defined strategy will allow reconstruction processes to become a powerful tool for a transition toward a sustainable development model. Cities under pressure, extreme conditions that call for radical solutions and bold assumptions, are an extraordinary chance to identify, test, and apply the latest available technological advancements. It is fundamental to move away from a vision of sustainability as an easy slogan heralded as a panacea for all evils, and used as a screen for the inability to propose alternative development models. Technological advancements are too often seen as technocratic solutions capable of fixing all urban problems, without any regard for cultural specificities, and aiming at a total absence of political and social conflict [RACO AND SAVINI 2019]. The easiest example is perhaps the hegemony of the smart city debate [HALEGOUA 2020; YAMAGATA AND YANG 2020], with the goal of transforming urban spaces into responsive environments where every behavior is observed, aided, or sanctioned by sensors and technologies. Smart cities hide under a utopian technocratic vision of the construction of urban spaces that transforms citizens into users and consumers, while "a true 'smart city' is not one that can do more with less—a great slogan for times of austerity—but one that is aware, and also proud, of its limitations and imperfections, one that respects minorities and their harmless diversities and does not violate the rights of its inhabitants, including that of using the city" [MOROZOV AND BRIA 2018]. Technological applications in urban environments thus become tools for establishing coherence and a forced order within an urban landscape, which is by its very nature incoherent [LEFEBVRE 1968].

The necessary sustainable transition, however, can be guided by a possible alternative model, often poorly considered but still highly operational: it is the historic city, the scraps of preindustrial urban fabric, that stubbornly have come down to us—crossing, certainly not unscathed, centuries of urban history. It is clear that the preservation of the historic city is the first step toward a sustainable future, but it is certainly not enough. Indeed, it is necessary to develop practices capable of making historic cities the active operational engines of the construction of the contemporary city

(MURATORI 1960). The system of historical cores shows the possibility of investing in tangible and intangible assets that cannot be delocalized. It is an actual and physical contrast between local diversity and the indifferent homologation of globalization (MARINO 2021).

Historical cores cannot, and should not, be copied in terms of their materials and architectural forms; instead, they must be considered as precious lessons on a quest for a dynamic equilibrium of physical resources and community needs. The historic city is a model because it testifies that processes of refinement through trial and error can lead to urban quality solutions; and also because, as pointed out by David Harvey, "the question of what kind of city we want cannot be divorced from the question of what kind of people we want to be, what kind of social relations we seek, what relations to nature we cherish, what style of life we desire, what aesthetics values we hold" (HARVEY 2012). Historic urban environments are not simply physical artifacts; they make visible and embody the cultural and social models that permitted their creation. How to achieve in a relatively short time the resilience refined over the centuries by the historic city, without passing through generations of disease, hunger, error, and dramatic naivety, remains the main operational challenge of reconstruction processes (ALBRECHT AND MAGRIN 2015), an effort that tries to overlap and synchronize for short stretches what Fernand Braudel called the deep and superficial currents of history (BRAUDEL 1998).

We certainly know that "the (historic) city is at once the laboratory of environmental reconstruction and the guarantee that an undertaking of this sort is feasible, providing that the particular city dates from the not too remote past and continues at least partially to function" (BENEVOLO 1993), and again that "the still inhabited historical cores become a concrete demonstration that the post-liberal model is not inevitable; yesterday it was possible to build a different and still functioning environment, tomorrow it will be possible to build a new environment that respects the same essential values, of which the inhabited areas are already ideally part. Therefore (the historical cores) do not interest us because they are beautiful or historical but because they indicate a possible future transformation of the whole city in which we live" (BENEVOLO 1984). A manifesto toward a truly sustainable transition.

4_2   ## THE LEAP FORWARD

The historical cores are the key reference for the urban qualities desired in the reconstructed city, but they must be adjourned to the latest technological evolutions available in the global scenario in order to provide viable solutions for the complex challenges posed by cities under pressure. Only a reconstruction able to match the qualitative character of the historic city with the highest possible quantitative performance will allow a true sustainable transition. However, a third factor must be considered: the social

4_ SUSTAINABLE TRANSITION

FEATURES OF THE HISTORICAL CORE

•

A. Materials. The selection of construction materials in historical cores has been done taking into consideration multiple concurring factors: available natural resources, the small dimension of supply chains, skills of local labor, and technological capacities.

B. Event city. Public spaces in historical cores are easily adaptable to different uses. Temporary function can emerge and disappear with spontaneous or planned organizations and gatherings, a capacity to continuously generate new meanings and possibilities.

C. Commercial areas. In current urban environments, commercial areas are detached from housing and other functions, while in the historical cores they are directly linked to public spaces and private living areas acting as a diaphragm and mediation space.

D. Resilience. The slow process of trial and error that has enabled a refinement of technological and architectural solutions makes historical cores resilient to changes and easily modifiable in the case of extreme events, allowing an ecological relationship with the surrounding environment.

E. Multifunctional public space. Giambattista Nolli's Pianta Grande di Roma of 1748 showed continuity in public accessibility and a use of internal and external spaces, a deep character of the historical core that can still be witnessed today.

F. Density. Historical cores, regardless of their history, geographical location, or climate and cultural specificities, have on average a density (calculated as built square meters over total area) between 2.3 and 2.9; the same data calculated for urban sprawl is around 0.8 and 1.5.

FILLING THE TECHNOLOGICAL GAP: THE LEAP FORWARD

PRE-DISASTER

Response
POST-DISASTER

The scheme shows the period of adoption of selected technologies by cities in developed and developing countries: the distance between the dots is defined as a technological gap. In standard conditions, the gap is closing given the widespread global availability of the latest technological evolutions. However, major disasters tend to significantly increase the gap in very short time frames. The proposed strategy aims at a major technological leap forward by seeing the reconstruction process as a chance to immediately apply the most advanced available technologies, regardless of the current level of development.

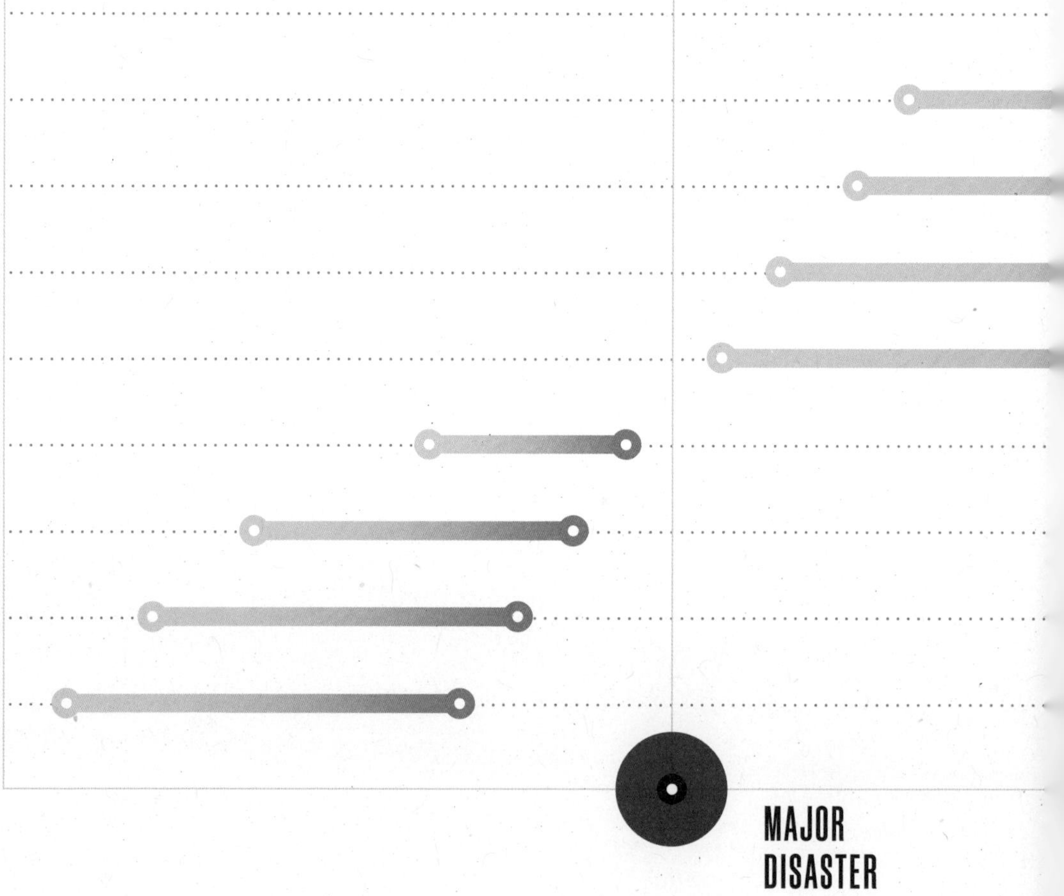

MAJOR
DISASTER

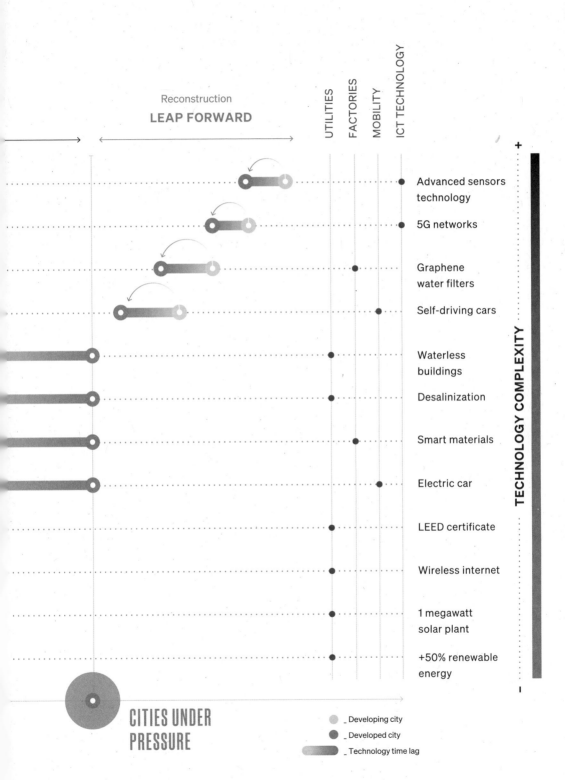

Reconstruction
LEAP FORWARD

UTILITIES
FACTORIES
MOBILITY
ICT TECHNOLOGY

Advanced sensors
technology

5G networks

Graphene
water filters

Self-driving cars

Waterless
buildings

Desalinization

Smart materials

Electric car

LEED certificate

Wireless internet

1 megawatt
solar plant

+50% renewable
energy

TECHNOLOGY COMPLEXITY

+

‒

**CITIES UNDER
PRESSURE**

_ Developing city
_ Developed city
_ Technology time lag

impact of technology and the different level of availability and adaptation in different geographical and social conditions [ARCHIBUGI AND PIETROBELLI 2003; UNCTAD 2006]. A scientific and technological discovery is always socially constructed and always culture-bound, but it is never simply true, and technological transfer is never a purely neutral process [HEADRICK 1988].

Territories prone to violence, social conflict, or recurrent natural disasters are often subject to a technological time lag caused by the impossibility of developing or accessing the most updated technological advancements. Reconstruction can become an occasion to immediately access and fruitfully exploit the latest global technologies, making a leap forward without the necessity to pass through different evolutive phases. It is vital to be aware and control the social impact of technologies that might enhance violence or inequality [PIERSKALLA AND HOLLENBACH 2013; BAILARD 2015] or, on the contrary, to facilitate collective action problems and improve in-group coordination and cooperation [POBLET 2011; RAMSBOTHAM ET AL. 2011; MANCINI 2013]. Within the proposed strategy, four main fields can allow technology to become a precious tool for sustainable transition:

a.

UTILITIES

.

Providing energy and water through integrated renewable sources and smart distribution systems in a vision that aims for a wise management of commons [OSTROM 1990; DE ANGELIS 2017] for the benefit of a whole community rather than for individual customers.

b.

FACTORIES

.

Producing light building materials on site that maximize secondary materials derived from occurred destructions and that involve the local population in transformation processes and self-construction mechanisms. The production of materials, while having the lowest possible impact on resources, should be inserted into a vision that reconnects productive cycles and construction types by working on sets of variation and customization within a unitary settlement principle.

c.

MOBILITY

.

Assuming that the future reconstructed city will employ a "mobility as a service" philosophy [HENSHER ET AL. 2020], banning cars from urban cells in favor of low-impact, self-driving vehicles [MOSS 2015]. The transformation of low-quality infrastructural nodes [FOURIE ET AL. 2020] in public space liberated from traffic will significantly increase the density and compactness of urban environments.

d.   **ICT TECHNOLOGIES**

ICT technologies have already been tested and applied in early warning systems (ASIMAKOPOULOU AND BESSIS 2010), but their capacity to empower the different actors in the reconstruction processes is yet unexplored. The bottom-up strategy can benefit from the definition and development of tools, such as e-learning systems, data-gathering and data-sharing platforms, online tutorials, ownership rights definition and GPS tracking, 3D visualization and augmented reality (AR), et cetera.

The horizon for the application of technologies allowing a true leap forward toward a sustainable transition involves the maximization of local employment favoring distributive policies (MATHEWS 1999); the definition of the dynamic equilibrium of urban space can be obtained through a mosaic of small-scale construction firms and service providers. In order to create employment on a large scale, labor-intensive sectors must be favored (IZUMI AND SHAW 2015), automation must be integrated with irreplaceable human action (SRNICEK AND WILLIAMS 2015), and innovation must be tamed by the careful respect of natural and social resources (BOOKCHIN 1989). "We want to accelerate the process of technological evolution. But what we are arguing for is not techno-utopianism. Never believe that technology will be sufficient to save us. Necessary, yes, but never sufficient without socio-political action. Technology and the social are intimately bound up with one another, and changes in either potentiate and reinforce changes in the other" (SRNICEK AND WILLIAMS 2017).

4_3   DECENTRALIZED MODEL

Reconstruction is a chance to define and build a development system that moves away from a technocratic vision of technology and embraces local self-development (MAGNAGHI 2010), a radical modification of current global paradigms that maximizes the decentralization of decision-making and urban production processes. Extreme events allow territorial management systems to be tested, in which policy decisions are made by groups gathered in assemblies with variable dimensions (region, city, neighborhood, etc.) and specific functions, a libertarian municipalism exposed by Murray Bookchin as a fluid conceptual framework, conscious that "how work should be planned, what technologies should be used, how goods should be distributed are questions that can only be resolved in practice. The maxim 'from each according to his or her ability, to each according to his or her needs' would seem a bedrock guide for an economically rational society, provided to be sure that goods are of the highest durability and quality, that needs are guided by rational and ecological standards, and that the ancient notions of limit and balance replace the bourgeois marketplace imperative of 'grow or die'" (BOOKCHIN 1991).

MODELS OF DECENTRALIZED ADMINISTRATION

The map on this page illustrates the current administrative model: the territory is subdivided into municipalities, with different features in different countries, that manage large parts of the services (energy, waste, construction permits, etc.). A few specific functions (water, biodiversity, etc.) can be entrusted to larger organizations, such as the unions of municipalities or government authorities. The alternative model proposed on the next page shows how the FOCJ concept can be applied to the territory: the

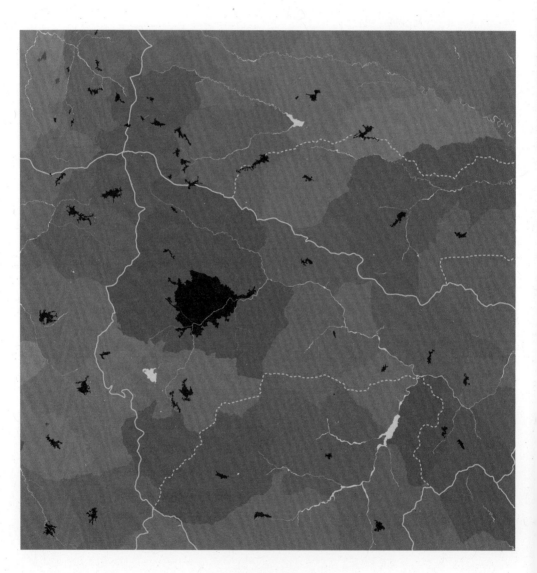

MUNICIPALITIES
Current adiministrative model

4_ SUSTAINABLE TRANSITION

management of resources can be
carried out through competing
organizations that overlap and
act simultaneously in the same
locations.

● _ Historical core
● _ Administrative borders
● _ River basin
● _ Waterways
● _ FOCJ

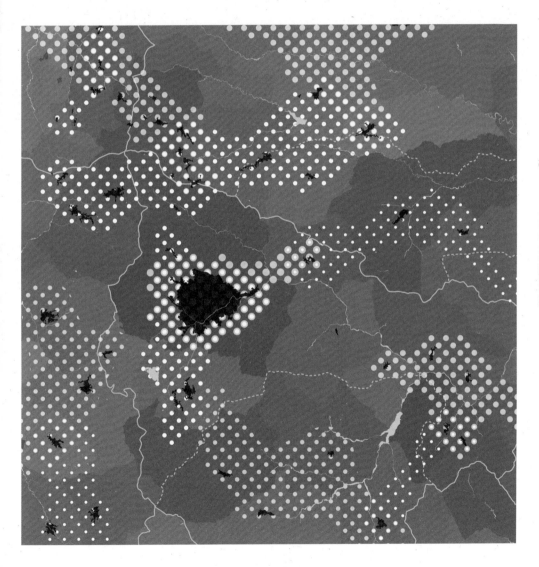

4_ SUSTAINABLE TRANSITION

FOCJ CONCEPT
Alternative model

If the utopia of a world completely organized in small autonomous units appears unattainable, then certainly the construction of systems in which small-scale functional democratic bodies are governed by fully participatory assemblies and dialogue with larger-scale representative systems [DAHL 1990] seems to be the only possible solution to solving the current detachment of resources and production, communities and bureaucracies, territories and economies; and to tracing a path toward a "cosmopolitan democracy" [ARCHIBUGI 2009]. The progressively growing importance of transnational governments and the global awareness of the need to jointly tackle global challenges beyond national borders [HELD AND MCGREW 2002] transform nation-states into subjects whose decision-making capacity is questioned. Neither national nor transnational bodies are capable of managing the complex entanglement of issues that characterize urban metamorphosis. Instead, this can be entrusted to self-government bodies placed in relationship and dialogue with representative systems, with the aim of widening the spaces of individual and collective autonomy [CASTORIADIS 2001] and of partially solving the issue of full inclusion [HABERMAS 1998].

Current technologies allow a level of global connectivity that provides the possibility of continuous decentralization and aggregation on the basis of transitory interests between intersecting and overlapping groups [KHANNA 2016]. It is a condition well understood by the economists Bruno Frey and Reiner Eichenberger, who devised a system called Functional, Overlapping and Competing Jurisdictions (FOCJ) [FREY AND EICHENBERGER 1996, 1999; FREY 1994], a valuable tool for reconstruction processes. In a FOCJ, the administration of a certain service (mobility, water management, waste disposal, etc.) is guaranteed by voluntarily established associations that act with a single purpose, without clearly belonging to a defined territory. The individual functional units are overlapping and competitive, trying to attract the preference of individual citizens or entire communities. The reconstruction laboratories can operate as FOCJ, enabling one to attend to the will of the communities and to quickly experiment with and verify innovative ideas. The implementation of the FOCJ system makes it possible to form transient groups that coagulate around the preference for a certain factor (materials, self-construction, credit models, etc.) to verify the positive or negative implications of its application and steer its scale-up process.

4_4   ADAPTIVE CIRCULARITY

The defined fields for technological development are not to be considered as separate parallel elements but rather as a group of concurring factors working toward the common goal of sustainable economic, social, and urban transition. Reconstruction can be the chance to construct positive cycles that tend to join different design scales and subjects, thus reconnecting the production of urban spaces to the complex entanglement of technical and societal factors that define them. The definition and control of a settlement's principles and of its possible evolutive trajectories can be matched with the individuation and development of appropriate technologies (SCHUMACHER 1973), both in terms of sustainable transformation of natural resources and enrichment of social capital (PUTNAM 2000). Building construction can be linked to material production and constructive techniques in a process that aspires to the definition of circular models interconnected with each other at different scales.

Agricultural production, energy provision, water management, transformation mechanisms, industrial processes, and city-making can be imagined as crossed rings where intervention into a single element can trigger major changes in other parts of the mechanism. Technologies that require the smallest possible amount of external support should be favored, not in an anti-historical autarkic vision but in a process of maximization of local development (SACHS 1974) that matches large-scale knowledge and information networks with small-scale territorial and urban transformations. "It is therefore necessary to address the definition of rules for human settlements that do not require any external support for durable self-production. Hence the need to develop the concepts of 'local' and 'self-development' which underline the need to affirm a culture of self-government and care for the territory that is able to overcome the reliance of sustainable development to technological machines or heterodirect economies, through the reconquest by the inhabitants of the wisdom of production of environmental and territorial quality" (MAGNAGHI 2010). Technology becomes useful for development only in a vision capable of linking it to ecological and sustainable ethical guidance that guarantees its use as a means and not an end. The final goal is the definition of a development model capable of providing a safe and qualitative built environment through the capacity to continuously control the fluidity of urban metamorphosis by using technologies as indicators and boundaries of a wide range of chances.

Circular productive and technological systems can be defined in the abstract, but their application is strictly linked to the possibility of adapting the concepts to the specific conditions of each area involved in extreme events. Utilities, factories, and mobility choices are bound to the specificity of each social, economic, cultural, geographical, and historical condition, thus requiring a flexible management system (ELLRAM ET AL. 2022). On the one side, the presence of a reconstruction laboratory ensures compliance with the needs and aspirations of the local communities, but on the other, technical decisions might require a level of knowledge that exceeds that of local assemblies. The adaptation of technological means can be conducted through the transformation of resources and objectives in terms of input and output that can shrink and expand the conceptual model and its spatial implications. Design experts are called on to continuously define the porous borders of these processes, accounting for their impact on the modification of urban environments. Rather than a specific spatial configuration, the design aims for the definition of a fluid mechanism that can be continuously adapted and recalibrated while maintaining the clarity of its final goal.

4. SUSTAINABLE TRANSITION

WATERSCAPE

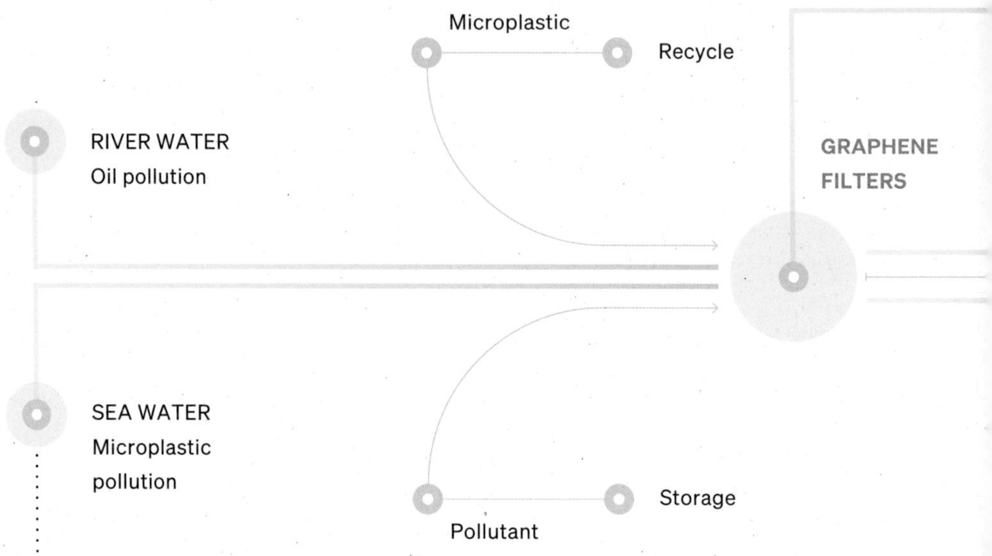

Microplastic

Recycle

RIVER WATER
Oil pollution

GRAPHENE
FILTERS

SEA WATER
Microplastic
pollution

Pollutant

Storage

4_ SUSTAINABLE TRANSITION

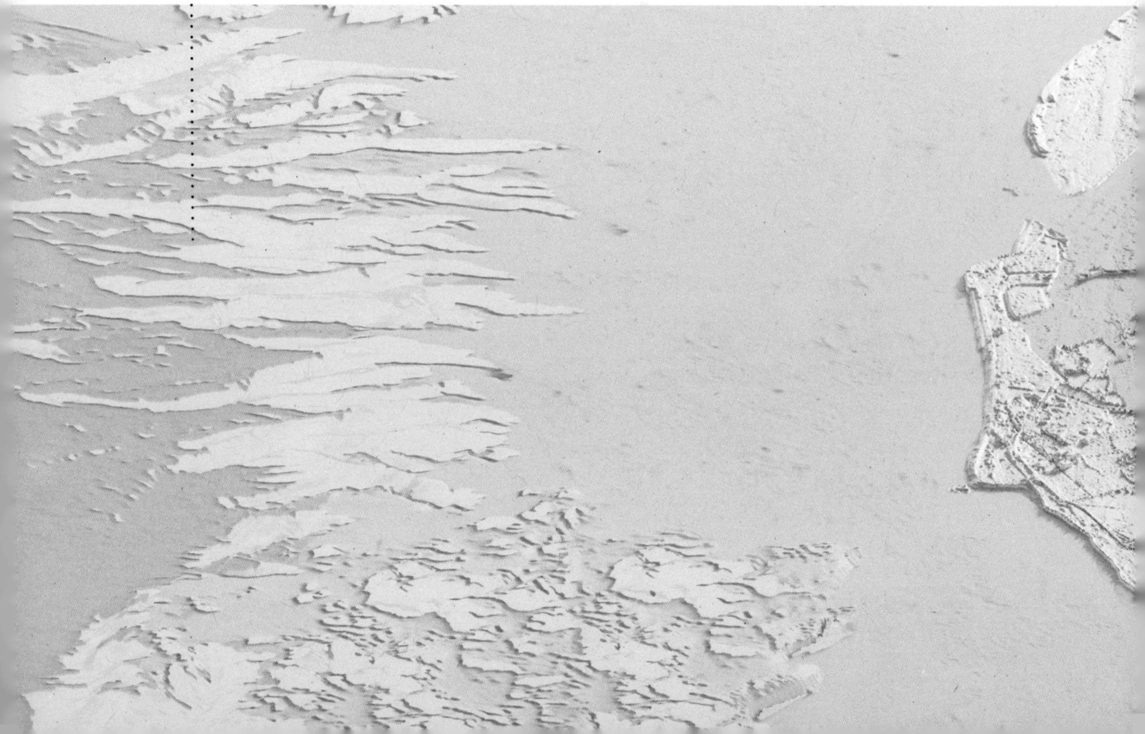

Any kind of human settlement or productive cycle is based on the availability of clean water, so today climate change and pollution are often a major limitation to development in many areas of the world. Desalinization of sea water is a technology that can guarantee a large amount of clean water for drinking, sanitary use, production, and agriculture and can initiate major modifications of the territory and the urban environment.

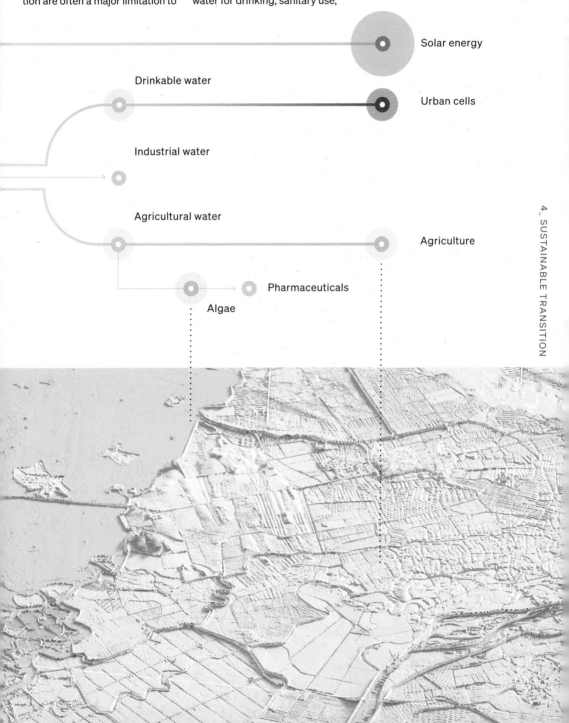

Solar energy

Drinkable water

Urban cells

Industrial water

Agricultural water

Agriculture

Pharmaceuticals

Algae

4. SUSTAINABLE TRANSITION

AGRISCAPE

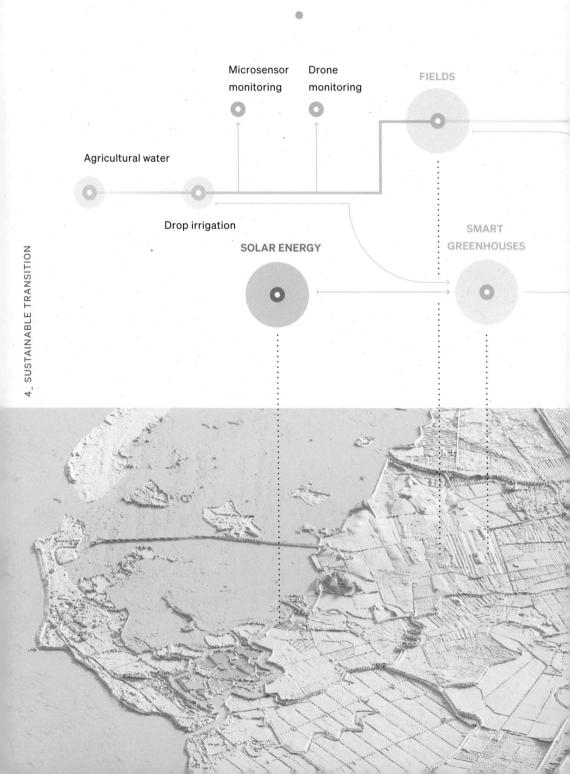

Microsensor monitoring

Drone monitoring

FIELDS

Agricultural water

Drop irrigation

SOLAR ENERGY

SMART GREENHOUSES

4_ SUSTAINABLE TRANSITION

The relationship between cities and the surrounding rural areas is often conflictual or nonexistent. However, the use of innovative tools, such as large-scale greenhouses or precision agriculture methods, can significantly increase productivity while minimizing the waste of resources. Technology can significantly shorten productive chains, while creating new employment opportunities and thus reconnecting the urban and rural dimensions.

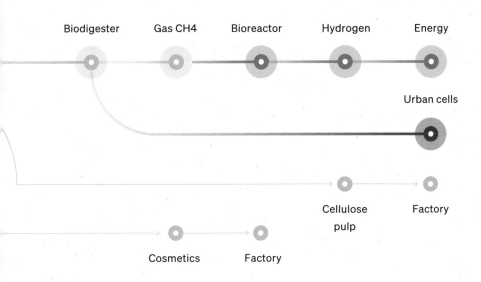

Biodigester   Gas CH4   Bioreactor   Hydrogen   Energy

Urban cells

Cellulose pulp   Factory

Cosmetics   Factory

4_ SUSTAINABLE TRANSITION

PRODUCTIVESCAPE

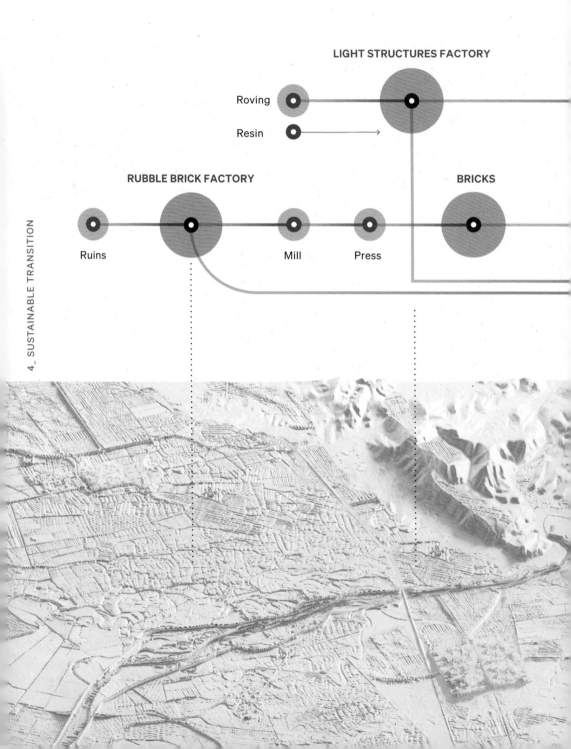

LIGHT STRUCTURES FACTORY

Roving

Resin

RUBBLE BRICK FACTORY

BRICKS

Ruins

Mill

Press

4_ SUSTAINABLE TRANSITION

Production and transformation processes need to find a new connection with local resources, in terms of both local community involvement and the use of on-site materials, thus significantly shortening productive chains and minimizing financial needs. Reconstruction should be based as much as possible on the recovery of destroyed buildings through processes of recycling and transformation of ruins using secondary raw materials.

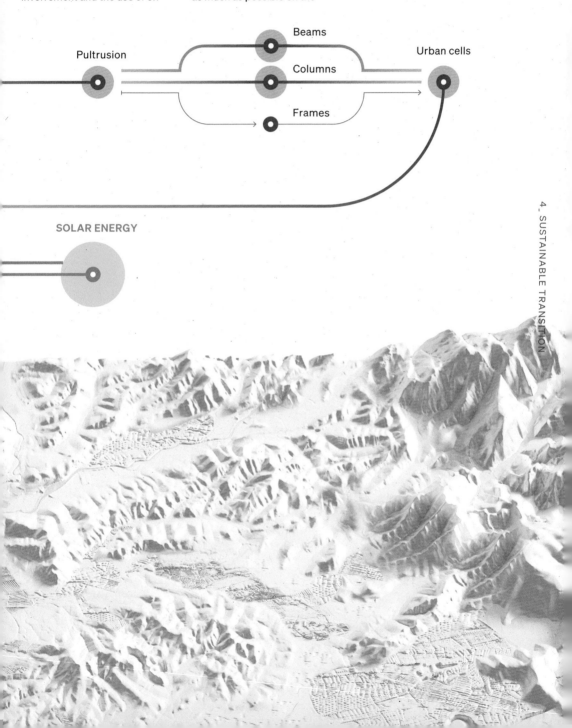

Pultrusion

Beams

Columns

Frames

Urban cells

SOLAR ENERGY

4. SUSTAINABLE TRANSITION

ENERGYSCAPE

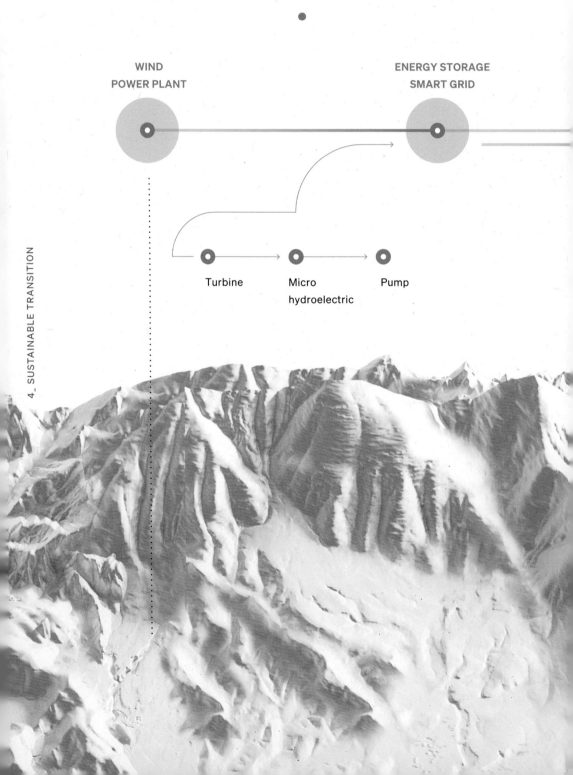

WIND
POWER PLANT

ENERGY STORAGE
SMART GRID

Turbine

Micro
hydroelectric

Pump

4_ SUSTAINABLE TRANSITION

Cities and territories involved in extreme events experience high levels of energy poverty with major problems in terms of supply and production. A level of energetic autonomy capable of guaranteeing basic services even in severe conditions is a central factor in reconstruction and can be achieved only through the diversification of sources, the maximization of renewable supply, more resilient to shock, and the increase in stand-alone systems.

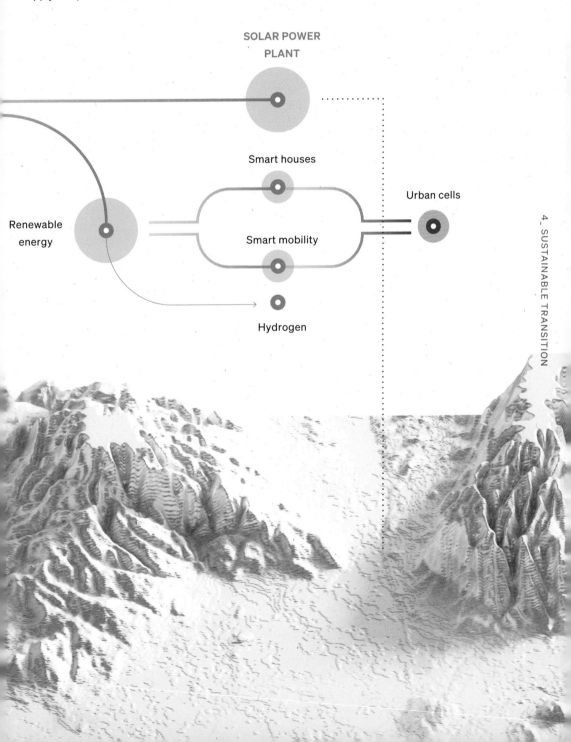

SOLAR POWER PLANT

Smart houses

Renewable energy

Smart mobility

Urban cells

Hydrogen

4 _ SUSTAINABLE TRANSITION

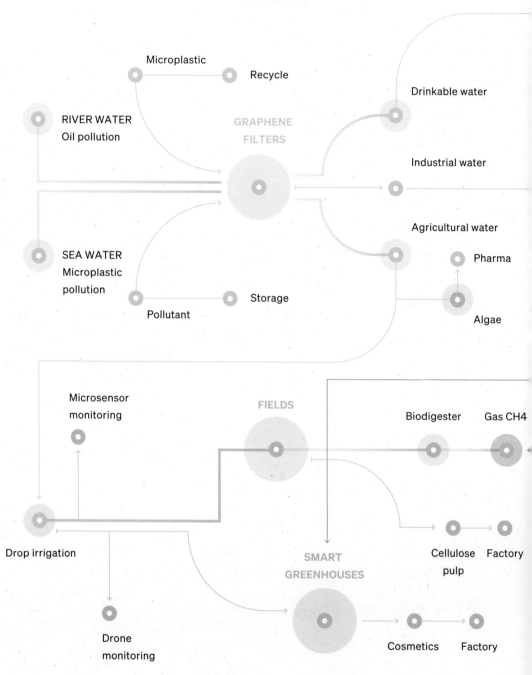

WATERSCAPE

Microplastic

Recycle

RIVER WATER
Oil pollution

GRAPHENE
FILTERS

Drinkable water

Industrial water

Agricultural water

Pharma

SEA WATER
Microplastic
pollution

Storage

Pollutant

Algae

Microsensor
monitoring

FIELDS

Biodigester   Gas CH4

Drop irrigation

SMART
GREENHOUSES

Cellulose
pulp

Factory

Drone
monitoring

Cosmetics   Factory

AGRISCAPE

ENERGYSCAPE

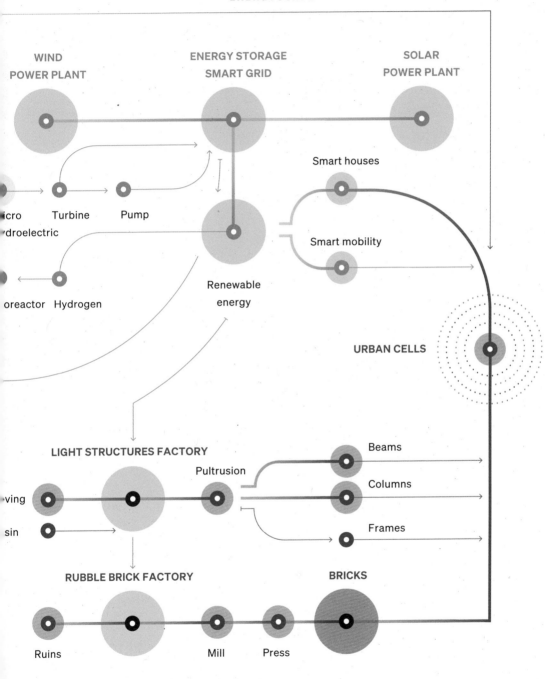

WIND
POWER PLANT

ENERGY STORAGE
SMART GRID

SOLAR
POWER PLANT

Smart houses

icro
droelectric

Turbine

Pump

Smart mobility

oreactor Hydrogen

Renewable
energy

URBAN CELLS

LIGHT STRUCTURES FACTORY

Pultrusion

Beams

Columns

ving

sin

Frames

RUBBLE BRICK FACTORY

BRICKS

Ruins

Mill

Press

PRODUCTIVESCAPE

5_

EXPLORATIONS

The on-site application of the cities under pressure mechanism will require a high capacity of adaptation to the unique economic, social, cultural, historical, and climatic conditions of each city and territory involved in extreme events. Conducting design explorations into the specific solutions required by each site facilitates a synthesis leading to the selection of the most appropriate tools capable of guiding the positive metamorphoses of the urban pattern. Each exploration assesses site conditions, defines the most pressing issues, and sets in motion the design process by defining suitable urban triggers and forecasting the consequent evolutions of the urban environment. Design variability allows one to observe the wide range of urban and architectural solutions.

SETTLEMENT PRINCIPLE AS A CHANCE FOR URBAN METAMORPHOSIS

•

Elisa Vendemini

↑

VENEZIA / ITALY

—

45°26'23''N 12°19'55''E

The city of Venice owes its worldwide fame to the aquatic land-scape from which it emerges. The lagoon with its network of ca-nals has allowed the protection of the urban environment from en-emy invasions for almost twelve centuries and still today attracts visitors from all over the world due to its uniqueness. A contin-uous negotiation between water and man has been evolving for centuries, but in recent years, it has been jeopardizing the very existence of the city. The year 2019 marked a record number of exceptional weather-marine events: the sea level exceeded 110 centimeters (the level at which 12 percent of the city is flooded) twenty-eight times and reached 189 centimeters on November 12, the second greatest extreme event since the acqua granda of 1966, which, with its 194 centimeters, started the global debate on the need to save Venice.

In addition to the increasing frequency of extreme events, there is a progressive reduction of services to citizens in favor touristic services and a relocation of management and administrative activities. These are all factors that have favored a sudden decrease in the resident population in the historic city, halved compared to 1966 and falling below the symbolic threshold of 49,999 in May 2022. Countering depopulation, enhancing the quality of living, and eliminating disastrous floods while preserving the environmental system and diversifying tourist monoculture are the most urgent objectives for present-day and future Venice. MOSE, a system of mobile sluice gates installed on the seabed of the port inlets of the lagoon to protect the city from high tides, is fully functional but not a definitive solution since the sudden rise of the average sea level will make it obsolete within a few decades.

The last significant urban changes in Venice date back to the Napoleonic era, and in the collective imagination the city appears immutable. In reality, however, there are areas of significant dimensions on the edge of the city which can be subject to strong changes. Areas that have lost the historical settlement principles where it could "image a spectrum of modern types of homes and quarters, not reproducing the standard of the international types, but trying to follow the peculiar needs of climate, of tradition, and wishes" (BENEVOLO 1976). It is possible to imagine a unitary design for these edges that responds to emerging critical issues and enhances local character. It is a coherent transformation, taking up the settlement principles that gave rise to the city: walls perpendicular to the canals, with an almost constant structural pace (19–31 Venetian feet corresponding to 6.60–10.75 meters) resulting from the size of the wooden trunks; covered spaces alternating with a hierarchy of public, semipublic, and private spaces that develop flawlessly without interruption.

The walls will manage the development of the new urban fabric, allowing a hooking system with various configurations; a controlled process that is open to varying conditions, an operation carried out in verifiable stages and in continuous evolution; a renewal that follows the urban form of the historic city as an ideal model but which updates its typological features, structural elements, and technological solutions.

5_ EXPLORATIONS

URBAN TRIGGERS IN POST-EARTHQUAKE RECONSTRUCTION

•

Chiara Semenzin

↑

LIMA / PERU

—

12°03'36"S 77°02'15"W

The reconstruction strategy in Lima, Peru, a city that is periodically involved in extreme earthquakes, starts by giving priority to repair over reconstruction and by determining the limit beyond which this should not be pursued. From this it is possible to structure a process that, setting out from the preservation of the urban fabric through the restoration of street layouts, applies principles of urban restoration for historical cores and an approach toward suburban areas that tends to align them to the morphological character of the consolidated urban fabric. Backgrounding each intervention is the constant dialogue with the local population, who are directly involved in the reconstruction choices. The restoration of damage to urban fabrics and individual buildings responds to the combined need to recover the affected heritage and rebuild the lost community identity. Post-earthquake reconstruction must also be structured rapidly in order to contain the economic impact of the catastrophe.

Among the succession of models proposed for post-earthquake reconstruction in Italy, the Friulian experience after the 1976 earthquakes offers suggestions and useful starting points for structuring a functional process to meet the immediate needs of the population and to facilitate long-term economic recovery and social development of the damaged territory. Breaking with centralized management models, Friuli's reconstruction was structured as a horizontal process in both governance and physical implementation. Alongside a bottom-up system, interventions are standardized and applicable at the scale of the building. Through the individual interventions, the damaged urban fabric is confirmed and reconstructed according to the pre-earthquake volumetric proportions.

The intervention strategy distinguishes between inside and outside historical cores. In the historical cores, the post-earthquake reconstruction process starts with the cataloging of the on-site rubble, indispensable for the reconstruction of the damaged heritage. This is followed by a fundamental phase of damage analysis and the collection of available documentation that leads first to the repair of the damaged buildings and then to the reconstruction of the destroyed ones. In the areas outside of the historic fabric, reconstruction also becomes a corrective to existing criticalities, triggering an urban transformation that aims at densifying and concentrating the urban fabric toward the characteristics of the historical core and safeguarding the territory from uncontrolled urban sprawl. In areas with high seismic or hydrogeological risk, reconstruction is to be replaced by demolition and displacement to areas in denser urban fabrics.

Once the founding features of the damaged fabric have been identified, the project develops a diffuse structural grid as a trigger for the implementation of individual interventions. The same structural principle may be used to repair works, a process that is to be started immediately after the damage has been assessed. In the areas to be reconstructed and densified, the buildings will be developed according to high-quality standards given by the new structural grid that permits the setting up of an innovative and technological infrastructure.

5_ EXPLORATIONS

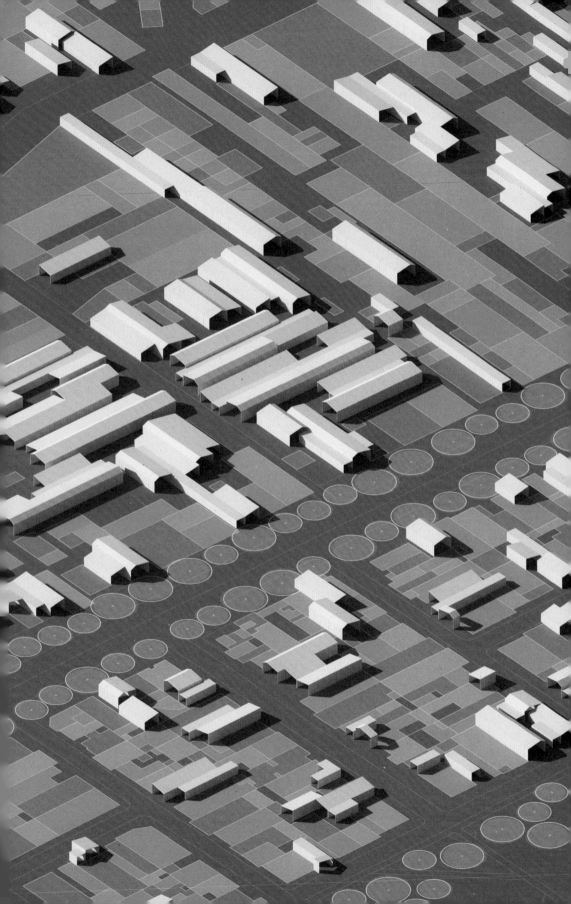

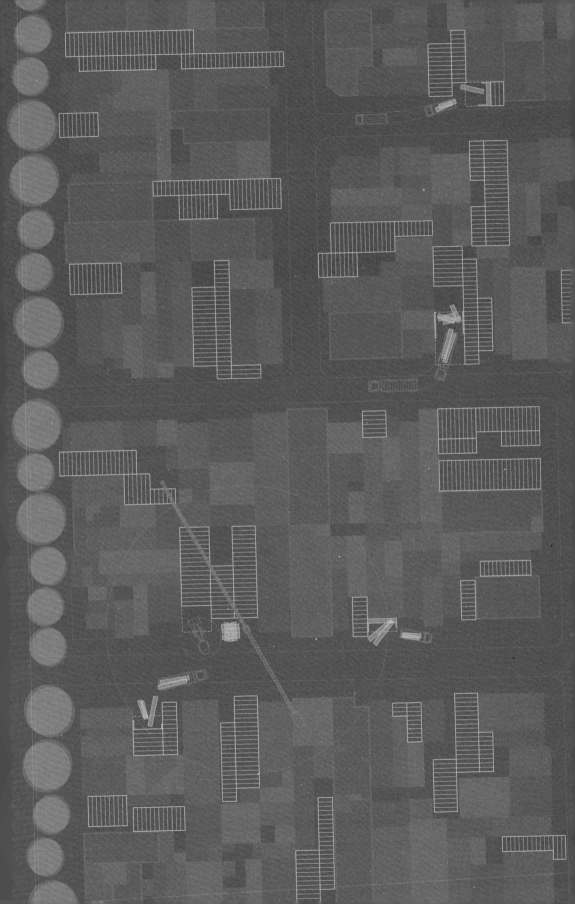

THE RECONSTRUCTION OF SMALL SIZE

●

Giulia Piacenti

↑

ALEPPO / SYRIA

—

36°12'07''N 37°10'03''E

Following Syria's industrial development concentrated in large cities and a drought that affected the state between 2006 and 2010, the city of Aleppo expanded very quickly with massive movements from rural to peri-urban areas. The shape of the new settlements reflected the ethnic and religious divisions of the population, forming a decentralized model that opposed the centralizing will of the government. The 2010 report "Aleppo Diverse Open City" by the Berlin-based studio Uberbau, commissioned to draw up a development scenario for the year 2025, describes Aleppo from a social point of view as strikingly multifaceted, a result of its history.

The variety of civilizations of the oldest continuously inhabited city in the world led to a highly organized social, religious, and economic structure. The constant invasions and political instability forced inhabitants of the city to build cell-like quarters and districts that were socially and economically independent. Each quarter differed by the religious and ethnic characteristics of its inhabitants. This social plurality is evident in the current city structure, as each city quarter has a distinct role and quality. During the Syrian civil war, it was precisely from these peri-urban and informal settlements, excluded from prosperity for much too long, that the rebels' military offensive against Aleppo, seen not only as a center of power but also as strongholds of wealth for the old (Sunnis) and new (Alaouites) rich, began.

Today, with the end of large-scale military operations, it is possible to imagine and plan the future reconstruction of the city, starting precisely from the rebuilding of the previous system of neighborhoods, pursuing an idea analyzed and devised by a vast number of twentieth-century planners: the cellular city. The cellular city is an alternative idea to the big city and represents a design where a large-scale "organic" vision absorbs the various small urban units, and where the reshaping of problems to minimum terms accomplishes large-scale control. The neighborhood offers better conditions for the inhabitants' lives because it deals inside its borders with urban, social, health, educational, ecological, political, administrative, and architectural issues, acquiring a certain degree of autonomy and autarchy.

New neighborhoods can also be physically separated by borders or strips of green to be easily identifiable in their acquired physical unity and to prevent the welding of their limits, searching for a balance between built and open space. Reconstructing a city through different neighborhoods helps to resolve ethnic, religious, and class divisions, provided that there are no significant differences in the distribution of resources, and allows the urban-rural division that characterized Aleppo before the war to be overcome. Reconstructing Aleppo according to neighborhoods can once again make Aleppo a city of civilization as it had been before the birth of Syria as a state, where a multicultural but aggregating power had ensured its development. Shaping a city made up of parts with their own urban, cultural, and administrative independence but connected to the historical core and each other by fast communication routes means shaping parts of a single unit. Aleppo can become an example of a new urban form born out of its past.

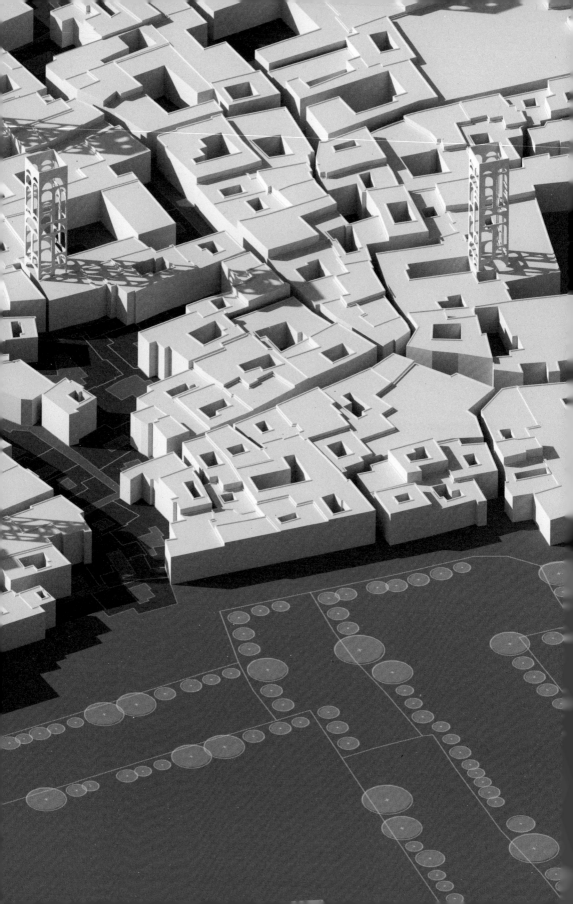

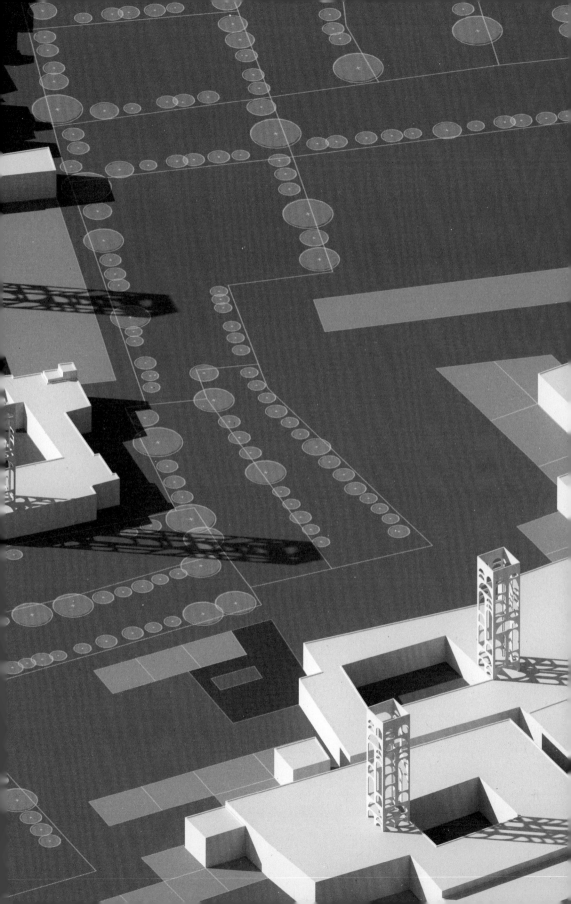

SOUKS AS URBAN CATALYSTS

•

Sabrina Righi

↑

MOSUL / IRAQ

—

36°21'23''N 43°09'50''E

Cities like Mosul in Iraq, systematically destroyed by violent waves of conflict, pose serious design questions related to the needs and opportunities of reconstruction. Urban warfare techniques show how easy it is to conquer a city when services are part of a big centralized system that can be easily controlled in a short time frame. Housing deficits make the community more fragile; when Mosul was taken by the Islamic State or Daesh in 2014, there was a lack of 46,000 housing units in the city. Mosul's growth started in the 1950s when it went from just 145,000 inhabitants to 1,377,000 in 2014. The failures in planning attempts led to the spread of informal settlements with no services and infrastructures, greatly favoring social conflict.

The city grew along big commercial streets that are between 20 and 30 meters wide and surrounded by big parking lots, thus losing proportions, quality of space, and the social role they had in the historical core. Reconstruction calls for a strategy that can remedy the lack of houses, services, and community spaces, while stopping the horizontal growth of the city that increases costs for new infrastructures. Interventions need to start from community spaces so as to reestablish facility buildings, promote economic growth, and provide a better quality of life.

In Middle Eastern cities, the center of public life and commerce is the souk, a system of covered streets flanked by businesses that spread into the tissue of the city, holding together institutional and facility spaces as the typical courtyard buildings. Souks have both a climatic and a structural role in the architecture of the city: they work as protection from sunlight and maximize internal airflow, are the structure along which buildings grow, and define a strong hierarchy of public and semiprivate streets that regulate functions and flows inside the city. The souks grew along the main streets that led to the city gates; then from the souk a second layer of internal streets branches off, surrounding groups of houses and ending in closed streets with private access to the single properties, defining subgroups of private houses inside the neighborhoods.

Articulated in a bottom-up process, increased and developed over time, the design aims to define and guarantee accessible public spaces through commercial and facility buildings that can trigger the reconstruction of private spaces, thus enhancing not only economic but also social development. New community and facility buildings will emerge in areas with destroyed buildings and along the width of big highways: they will have the same structure, designing a unique and integral system made of covered pedestrian paths and courtyards. This system can regulate and support the reconstruction of houses by owners and private investors inside an overall concept for the future city: the linear structures of souks will establish new borders for houses to be built using the same technology, sewing up the damaged urban fabric and densifying it. Souks, by changing the role of big highways, will permit the hierarchization of flows, distinguishing between commercial pedestrian paths, light mobility, streets, and semiprivate residential areas and hence guiding growth.

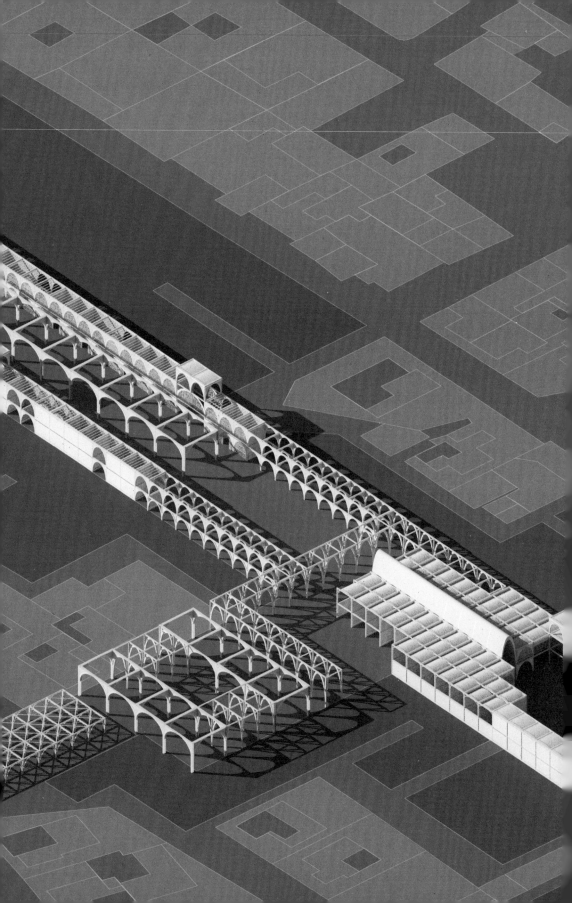

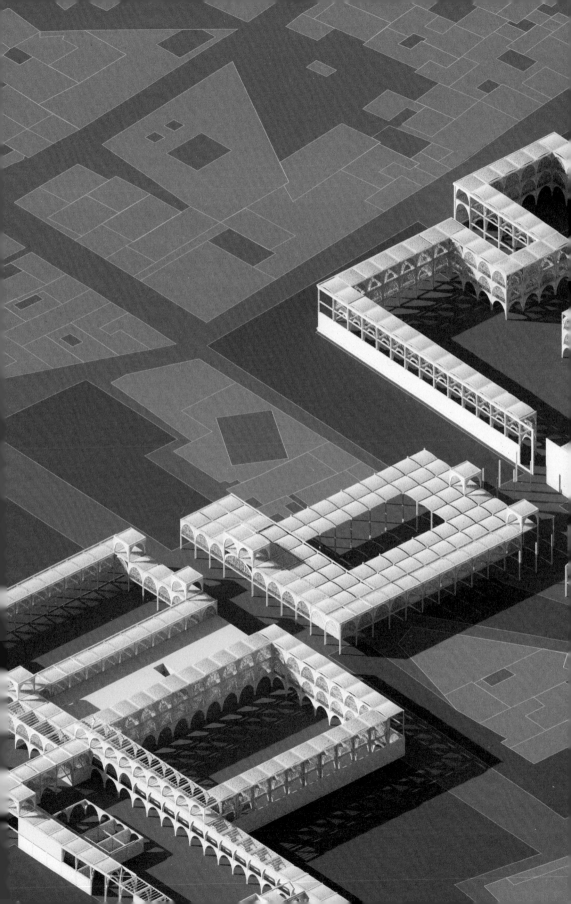

5_5

FROM HAZARD TO OPPORTUNITY: THE CONTROLLED FLOODING STRATEGY

•

Andrea Fantin

↑

NILE DELTA / EGYPT

—

31°24'03''N 30°24'53''E

5_ EXPLORATIONS

In the Nile Delta, the rise of the mean sea level, the subsidence process, and the gradual increase of the saline wedge will cause a considerable loss of agricultural land by the year 2100. It is necessary to design a new self-sufficient circular model switching from agriculture to aquaculture. Transformation of the agricultural fields into ponds and reuse of river sediments for the construction and repair of embankments are just some of the local and punctual actions adopted by the project. The strategy of controlled flooding requires punctual, short-timing, and economically sustainable actions which follow the large-scale, irreversible territorial transformation step by step.

"The last seven years have been the hottest ever recorded. We are rapidly approaching dangerous tipping points for human health and safety, ecosystems, property and infrastructure." These words were repeated over a thousand times at the COP27 held in Egypt in November 2022. Media outlets, experts, and scientists are reporting dramatic facts about the climate change effect. Even some of the major worldwide broadcasting services have dedicated specific channels to the ongoing disastrous effects of climate change on our planet.

Focusing on water, the ongoing increase of global mean temperature highlights two main outcomes: first, sea level rise (SLR) affecting the coastlines and delta areas; second, a high risk of drought or prolonged periods of drought. Essentially, dry regions get drier and wet regions get wetter (HELD AND SODEN 2006), hence the exemplification of two opposite but correlated scenarios: too much water and too little water. In numbers, the likely rise in global mean sea level by 2100 fluctuates between 0.55 and 1.01 meters correspondingly, based on low and very high greenhouse gas emissions scenarios.

The key point here is the spiraling gap between a simplified data fetching process due to high technology advancement and growing public interest, on the one hand, and the complexity behind the real spatial meaning of the data per se, on the other. Despite a vast offer of web mapping tools to project impacts from coastal flooding or sea level rise, the spatial repercussions of such global phenomena are too big to be truly understood at the single and small human scales. First and foremost, the radical transformation of the landscape requires a full understanding of the whole water cycle, from mountain to sea, while the two extremities are merely starting points for physical chain reactions which drastically alter the landscape and the socioeconomic pattern associated with it.

The economic structure must be revised from the inexorable transformation of the landscape and not backward. From local to global and vice versa, the challenge is to equip each individual citizen with the necessary tools for deciphering the ongoing and inevitable spatial transformation. It is not just a "simple" preventive action; as a matter of fact, it is the indispensable cooperative action that aims to identify all those site-specific strategies that succeed in perpetually adapting and renewing the socioeconomic structure in accordance with the spatial transformation of the landscape.

5_ EXPLORATIONS

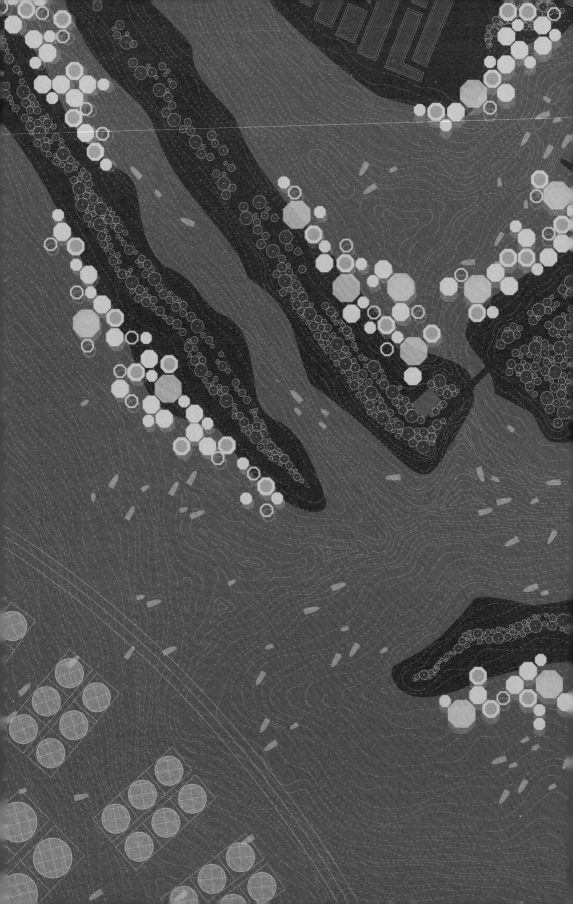

5_6

DESIGN WITHOUT
A DESIGN

•

Serena Pappalardo

↑

ACCRA / GHANA

—

5°36'53''N 0°12'21''W

5_ EXPLORATIONS

The site and services project proposed for the city of Accra in Ghana, where the first core housing experiments carried out by Otto Koenigsberger in the 1960s were located, envisages the construction of service blocks in connection with infrastructural systems. While the arrangement of the blocks outlines the overall urban system, the individual service centers are slowly absorbed by self-built houses. This design strategy overshadows the control of the formal dimension of architecture, but it proves to be an effective tool for the promotion of economic, social, and cultural development given its sensitivity to the housing needs of individuals within an overall community growth process. The reconstruction of urban areas affected by extreme events requires a concrete response to the rise in demand for housing and services, but it is also vital to ensure an urban environment capable of stimulating the community's socioeconomic growth.

The progressive development approach supported by the World Bank in the 1970s and 1980s for the construction of housing and neighborhoods in developing countries offers con-

crete examples that are still relevant today in promoting significant urban models. Compared to traditional low-cost public building programs, with centralized and hierarchical management that
requires a great deal of resources in the face of static and often
socially stigmatizing urban and architectural models, upgrading
and sites-and-services projects provide an alternative to individual strategic aspects of urban planning and minimal architectures
that can be expanded over time directly by the inhabitants.

The supply of plots equipped with essential infrastructures and of minimal mass-produced services has multiple
advantages: it allows for the inclusion of a wider range of benefi-
ciaries, it guarantees a better location for the categories that most
need to access the services of the city, and it allows the inhabitants to modify their homes according to specific needs and economic capacities.

The process of simplification of the architectural
form that leads to the definition of a minimum space, the need to
guarantee flexible and adaptable functional programs, and the
possibility of expansion over time are the principles of a "design
without a design," an architecture that attempts to influence the
formation of spontaneous settlement processes, accepting the
risk of losing its formal integrity and maximizing flexibility to meet
the needs of the users. The designer must be able to imagine how
the elementary and standardized architecture can be slowly modified and transformed by foreseeing an inaccurate but concrete
urban scenario. The trigger element that will generate the urban
form is a nucleus that houses essential services and that can expand horizontally or vertically depending on the pursued density.
It can be an enclosure that immediately defines the overall urban
form and whose interior spaces will be modified at a later time, or
be made up of complex construction elements.

5_ EXPLORATIONS

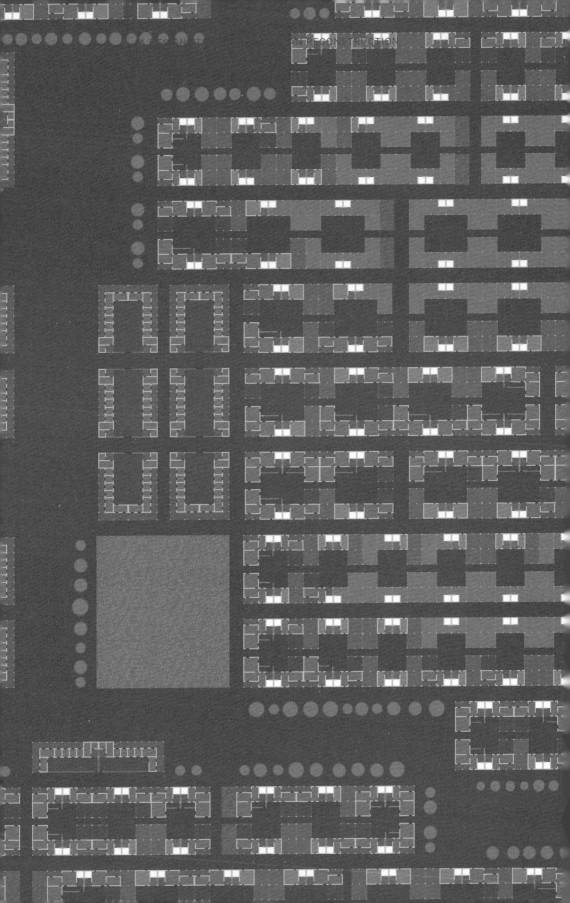

PIECEMEAL PLANNING
AT WORK

●

Marco Marino

↑

IRPIN / UKRAINE

—

50°31'7''N 30°14'23''E

The city of Irpin in the Kyiv Oblast—hit by Russian forces in March 2022—is characterized by a sparsely populated urban fabric made up of large residential complexes built in the Soviet period or in recent years, by commercial and tourist structures, and by an expansive network of single-family homes. The reconstruction of cities damaged by the Russian invasion of Ukraine is an opportunity to completely rethink and redesign urban settlements. Reconstruction can be managed by the presence of architectural devices capable of organizing urban development in space and time, in the case of Irpin a system of porticoes, artifacts that act as a new urban skeleton, a pivotal element for urban development.

The project involves the reconstruction of the city starting from the reshaping of the existing public space—streets, squares—and not from the reconstruction of individual buildings. The porticoes will be arranged in modules on the existing roads, invading the carriageway and significantly modifying its section. Initially the porticoes, arranged on public land, will serve as a roofing system for small temporary volumes intended for emergency housing, and over time they will become a hooking system for new constructions. The porticoes of Irpin will function as a regulator for urban development: each architectural structure, from homes to large public buildings, will be attached to them and, once the reconstruction is complete, will remain as a structuring part of the urban fabric, thus significantly increasing urban quality.

The new urban structure organized by the porticoes will enable the road section to be reduced from 20 meters to 8 meters, providing for a new road system. The porticoes will also enable the efficient distribution of services such as water and electricity, making the reconstruction process more efficient. The use of light and easily assembled construction elements will be decisive in the entire reconstruction project: beams and pillars can be produced with fiberglass, while infill walls can be made of high-performance insulating blocks, all dry-mounted without the use of cranes.

The general strategy with which the reconstruction of Irpin can be carried out is that of piecemeal planning, expressed by Ernst Gombrich in 1965, borrowed from the principles of "piecemeal engineering" postulated by Karl Popper. This type of intervention is based on the principles with which the preindustrial city was built. The urban quality resulting from the ancient city can only be obtained by approaching urban design as the result of continuous interventions that accumulate over time. The growth of a city can take place in small steps, which Gombrich defines as the "innumerable small and manageable ones," the articulation of which in time produces "the variety of visual variations" (GOMBRICH 1965) and therefore beauty. Piecemeal planning in Irpin leads to a reconstruction strategy of architectural microinterventions which together and in the short term will trigger urban macrotransformations. Piecemeal planning is a process, not a project, of controlled growth continuously sized to the needs of the community and its urban environment.

5_EXPLORATIONS

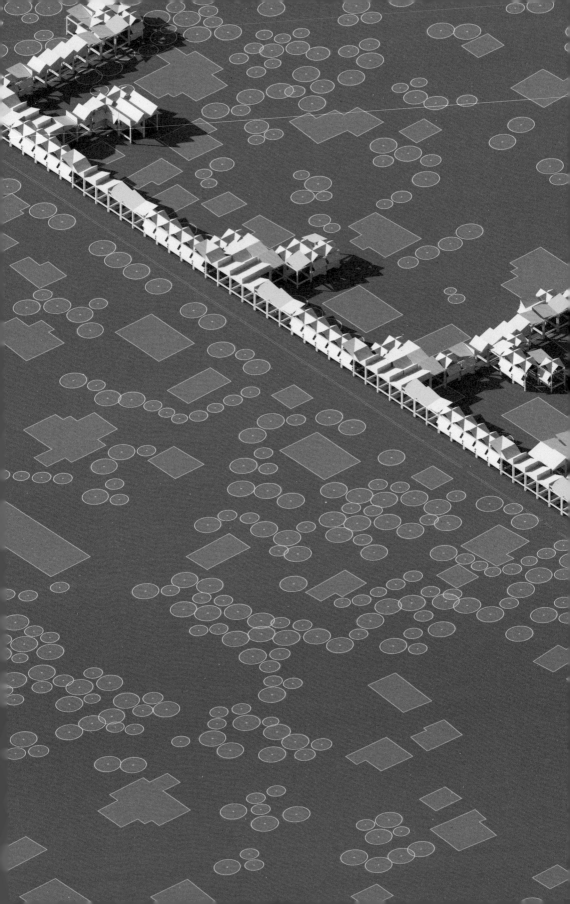

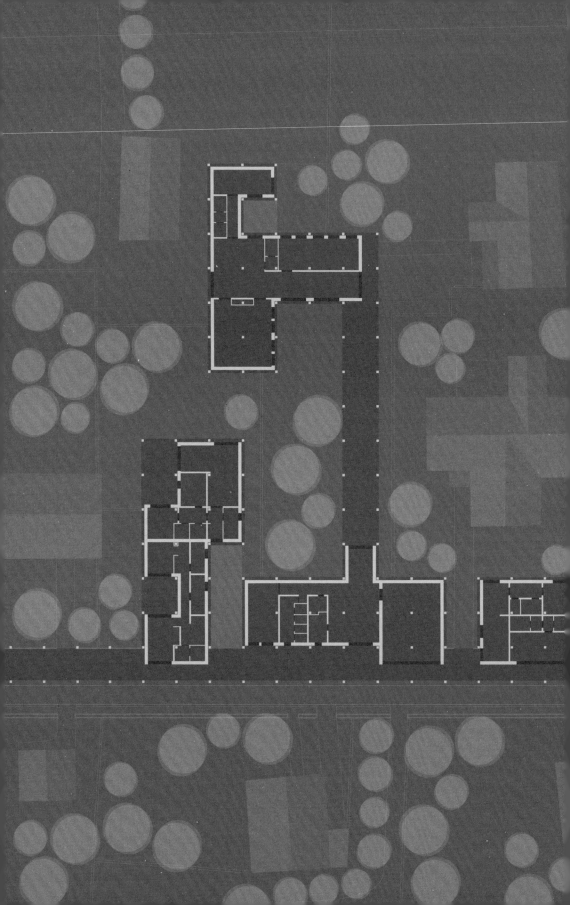

6.

DESIGN

Only a new design approach, with its specific design tools, may allow the fruitful application of the proposed strategy and its adaptation in different locations. Historical patterns, which on average amount to 5–7 percent of the total city, require an urban restoration approach, while postindustrial patterns, making up the remaining 95 percent, need processes of urban triggers capable of controlling urban metamorphosis through the definition of a public backbone and the guidance of private intervention using induced design mechanisms. The common trait is the necessity to define and apply a growing evolutionary mechanism that sees urban environments as fluid dynamic equilibriums to be continuously renegotiated.

DESIGN

•

6_1   **URBAN RESTORATION**

The design approach aiming toward the reconstruction of urban environments involved in extreme events is different in light of the nature of the destroyed patterns: historical cores and postindustrial cities require the application of specific design tools within a common strategic vision. On the one side, the goal is to conserve and ameliorate the existing urban form, while on the other, a different urban model must be devised and constructed, leading to a reconstructed city totally different from the pre-destruction one.

      The conservation policy of ancient cities, of the material and immaterial heritage of the inherited city, was conceived, from the very first experiments, in a unified and organic way. It was an "integrated conservation" [CHOAY 1992] that considered historical urban environments as single organisms, made up of buildings, open spaces, and inhabitants whose restoration was to be faced as a single object. The development of integrated conservation policies permits a definition of the urban restoration method that has proved to be valid and adaptable to different conditions. Born in Italy after World War II [CEDERNA 1961; CERVELLATI ET AL. 1977], it was adopted around Europe (Council of Europe 1975) and became a conceptual guide for large international organizations [BANDARIN AND VAN OERS 2012]. It is "a historically founded methodology for the study and modification of ancient and modern settlements" [BENEVOLO 2006]. The goal is the preservation of the physical body of the city, and of what was left of the social body that lived in it, so that they remained, as far as possible, united with each other. The technical and administrative intervention rules were identified in numerous experiments [ALBRECHT AND MAGRIN 2015], allowing a preservation the past, the possibility of continuity of use in the present, and a future for the inherited physical heritage. Societies, like individuals, can increase the possibilities of fruitful relationships only in the custody of the "long time," which is the time of the future and of the generations to come, in the awareness of duration and in the ability to remember, as an integral part of daily life. The historic city, its urban heritage, is the hereditary property of a society that gives it the sense of an indispensable intergenerational gift.

Urban restoration is at the same time a cognitive analysis and an operative action defined by a technical standard of four maps that guide all the modifications of the urban environment. The drafting of the set of drawings is the true design effort, which provides a blurred but coherent vision of the future city, while the design of single elements can be entrusted to a multitude of different architects, provided that they have understood and applied the overall intervention rules:

a.

TYPES

.

A map that identifies each building based on a list of building types defined in light of their form, size, and features. Types vary in each city based on local specificities, but the tracing ability of architectural types, which defines the history and consistency of the built environment, is accepted collectively, and it becomes a repeatable and comparable parameter in different situations.

b.

CONDITIONS

.

A map that identifies each building based on structural integrity and level of preservation of the horizontal and vertical surfaces. The conditions allow one to define for each building the scope of intervention that can range from simple renovation to recovery, through philological or typological restoration, up until complete modification with typological or volumetric substitution.

c.

FUNCTIONS

.

A map that identifies each building based on current function and possible future uses. The traditional mixed use that characterizes the historical city is to be preserved and revived, while a sufficient level of adaptability can allow unexpected and radical new interpretations.

d.

SURGERIES

.

A map that identifies the specific area of the urban pattern where interventions altering the current urban form may occur; the surgeries are configured as shadow projects that would need to be further designed but that once carried out will significantly ameliorate the overall environment.

6_ DESIGN

URBAN RESTORATION TOOLS

•

6_ DESIGN

↑ Building types

● _ Contemporary buildings ● _ Palaces

● _ Traditional houses ● _ Religious buildings

● _ Apartment buildings ● _ Public buildings

● _ Small palaces

● _ Good ● _ Housing

● _ Mediocre ● _ Facilities

● _ Bad ● _ Commercial

○ _ Footprint ● _ Tertiary sector

● _ Restoration

● _ Renovation

● _ Philological restoration

● _ Typological restoration

● _ Demolition of additions and philological restoration

● _ Demolition of additions and typological restoration

● _ Non-reconstruction

-- _ Development zones

↑ Levels of preservation

↑ Use

↑ Prescriptions and surgery

6_ DESIGN

**URBAN RESTORATION
TABLE**

●

The proposed operational frame-work is a 3D visualization of the possible interventions, built starting from the map of building types.

The transition from the analysis of the building type map to the operative prescriptions of the intervention model is carried out through the "implementation table," which crosses the building types with the intervention

↑ 3D pattern visualization

methods (on occupied, destroyed, or vacant areas) and the functions (current and possible in the near future). For each building type, the table indicates whether the different interventions are possible (★), not allowed (•) or possible at the ground floor (GF). The matching of typology with interventions is the main design operation of the entire urban restoration process.

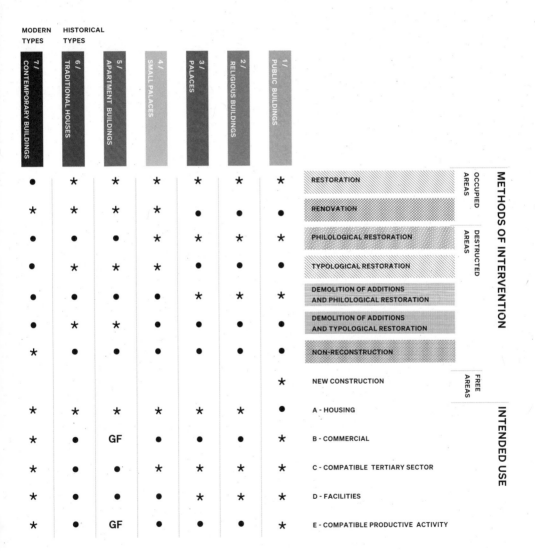

	MODERN TYPES	HISTORICAL TYPES							
	7 / CONTEMPORARY BUILDINGS	6 / TRADITIONAL HOUSES	5 / APARTMENT BUILDINGS	4 / SMALL PALACES	3 / PALACES	2 / RELIGIOUS BUILDINGS	1 / PUBLIC BUILDINGS		
RESTORATION	•	★	★	★	★	★	★	OCCUPIED AREAS	METHODS OF INTERVENTION
RENOVATION	★	★	★	★	•	•	•		
PHILOLOGICAL RESTORATION	•	•	•	★	★	★	★	DESTRUCTED AREAS	
TYPOLOGICAL RESTORATION	•	★	★	★	•	•	•		
DEMOLITION OF ADDITIONS AND PHILOLOGICAL RESTORATION	•	•	•	•	★	★	★		
DEMOLITION OF ADDITIONS AND TYPOLOGICAL RESTORATION	•	★	★	•	•	•	•		
NON-RECONSTRUCTION	★	•	•	•	•	•	•		
NEW CONSTRUCTION							★	FREE AREAS	
A - HOUSING	★	★	★	★	★	★	•		INTENDED USE
B - COMMERCIAL	★	•	GF	•	•	•	★		
C - COMPATIBLE TERTIARY SECTOR	★	•	•	★	★	★	★		
D - FACILITIES	★	•	•	•	★	★	★		
E - COMPATIBLE PRODUCTIVE ACTIVITY	★	•	GF	•	•	•	★		

6 _ DESIGN

Once the four maps have been drafted, a table providing all the possibilities of intervention allows the architect who will be designing the single elements to immediately access the full scope of choices in terms of uses, volumes, materials, and features. Urban restoration is configured as a single design of a single organism that is carried out by multiple hands in different times, continuously controlling the processes of urban metamorphosis.

6_2   URBAN TRIGGERS

Intervening in postindustrial urban patterns, often of a poor spatial quality and with poor technological performance, represents a vast majority of design efforts undertaken in reconstruction processes. The key is the establishment of a methodology capable of having the same intellectual and operational clarity of urban restoration. We define this approach as urban triggers: a design system capable of controlling urban metamorphosis in space and time through the definition and construction of elements that will trigger a positive modification of the urban environment. The result will not be a single solution but only a possible path, accepting that further modifications and adjustments will be made by different designers, with their specific emotions, sympathies, and knowledge (FRY AND DREW 1964). It is a humble acknowledgment of the fact that no final result exists, nor will one never be definable, and that the only credible proposal is the continuous renegotiation of a dynamic equilibrium, in which the urban settings at a given time are only a temporary concretization of one possibility within a finite but extremely large number of chances that can be limited only by the careful design of the triggers and the continuous steering of the multiple responses to them.

The system of urban triggers painstakingly seeks a mediation between the "long time," which describes the transformations of the environment and the city, and the "short time" of men and their forecast abilities. The times of metamorphosing cities and territories are long, and in the long term the construction and adaptation of urban systems is measured and has been measured historically. Time gives value to physical and knowledge stratification, to a culture of non-homogenizing space, which acts on the structural differences of the various metamorphosis mechanisms of physical reality. The "long time" then becomes a design culture, a culture of localized space, with all the strategic, administrative, and technical implications that this entails. The adaptation and improvement of the environment and the city become a process to be triggered.

Urban triggers attempt to adapt to the discipline of urban design, which Karl Popper defined as "piecemeal social engineering," criticizing the historicist approach to the definition and planning of future scenarios and arguing that the only form of social engineering that can be rationally justified is one which is small-scale, incremental, and continuously amended in the light of experience.

> The characteristic approach of the piecemeal engineer is this. Even though he may perhaps cherish some ideals which concern society "as a whole"—its general welfare, perhaps—he does not believe in the method of re-designing it as a whole. Whatever his ends, he tries to achieve them by small adjustments and readjustments which can be continually improved upon. . . . He knows that we can learn only from our mistakes. Accordingly, he will make his way, step by step, carefully comparing the results expected with the results achieved, and always on the look-out for the unavoidable unwanted consequences of any re-form; and he will avoid undertaking reforms of a complexity and scope which make it impossible for him to disentangle causes and effects, and to know what he is really doing (POPPER 1957).

Karl Popper's "piecemeal social engineering" is the conceptual base of Ernst Gombrich's chapter "The Beauty of Old Towns" in his seminal work *Reflections on the History of Art*. This volume can provide some further hints about the possibility of establishing a design approach which rather than leaning on deliberate planning creates the conditions for a fruitful, unplanned growth. Gombrich explains how the undeniable beauty and fascination of medieval towns is given by urban and architectural solutions "that evolved more or less as organisms do, through the survival of the fittest and the elimination of undesirable mutations" (GOMBRICH 1987) and that are unified under a common logic by the capacity of building types and construction techniques to limit the alternatives, and by the continuous possibility of alterations given to every generation to adapt to new requirements and new uses. A complex system built this way is naturally divided into subsystems, such that when one subsystem is modified, there is no cascading effect on others. This localizes the error and, as a result, makes the system, as a whole, more robust.

The traces left by Gombrich are intended not as romantic nostalgia of the past but as clues of contemporary design processes that must be able to re-propose, in the shortest possible time, operational tools that allow one to reach a fluid, dynamic equilibrium.

Urban triggers are a blurred definition of these design tools, allowing for democratic and shared community action guided by a collective intelligence to solve the complex entanglement of urban pressures. This is an anti-authorial, super-personal, and unselfconscious approach (ALEXANDER 1964) where the vain change for the sake of change is discouraged.

6_DESIGN

BACKBONES

Urban triggers operate in two main moments that tend to overlap, run forward, and catch up through adaptations: the public backbone led by communitarian action negotiated in the reconstruction laboratory; and the induced design carried out by private actors within a common framework of intervention. The public backbone must be shaped by urban designers as a system of hooks and suggestions capable of defining an open range of possibilities for the metamorphosis of the urban pattern through the fruitful mix of public and private spaces. The nature of the public backbone can be dramatically different in scale, type, and function and is the true keystone of the design process. Public backbones can belong to one or more of these broad categories, while unexpected solutions are always to be welcomed and embraced:

6_ DESIGN

a. **STREETS AND PATHS:** The ongoing transition in the mobility context with the "end of the car age" frees a significant amount of space that is currently occupied by vehicular traffic. Public intervention, which reshapes streets in size and nature, can initiate a complete rethinking of the related visual and user relationship [BANERJEE ET AL. 2012] and of the overall urban features in terms of density and diversity, allowing "eyes on the street" [KANIGEL 2016] to generate a rich social life full of chances, risks, and possibilities.

b. **CONSTRUCTION TECHNIQUES:** Construction choices suitable to economic, social, and cultural conditions and adequate to the current level of knowledge and skills can guide urban evolutions. Structural steps constitute the main set of measures of the urban environment, allowing one to unify under a common logic the multitude of design decisions to be made in different time frames. Construction techniques are fundamental in setting the pace for the modification of the urban form and directly involve local skills and labor, initiating positive economic cycles.

c. **PLOTS AND PROPERTIES:** Ownership structures remain active engines of urban modification even in the most severe cases of tabula rasa [BERNOULLI 1946]. The range of decisions from total maintenance of the grid to complete redrawing of the plots [HALLAJ 2018] foresees an infinite number of urban models, while the shape of the single plots suggests and implies specific architectural solutions.

d. **SERVICES:** The provision of basic services must be reestablished after extreme events in the shortest possible time frame, and in the longer framework issues such as water accessibility, sanitation, and energy can become precious drivers to attract or reduce density in specific parts of the urban pattern. Basic services can act as cores of incremental construction, while stand-alone mechanisms permit experimentation of innovative architectural and urban solutions.

e. **LEVEL OF PRIVACY:** Courtyards, gardens, patios, cloisters, and "chahar baghs" [NARNE AND BERTOLAZZI 2012] significantly enrich urban patterns and act as mediation spaces between private and public areas, providing varying levels of privacy suitable to different lifestyles and cultural specificities. The use of these devices can provide precious traces for the reconstructed city, while actively engaging users in appropriation and transformation mechanisms.

f. **COMMERCIAL AREAS:** Major commercial areas in selected parts of the contemporary city are allocated as depleted urban patterns of liveliness and complexity. Dislocated small commercial activities that are inserted organically into the urban environment can instead substantially increase the level of proximity [TORRE AND GALLAUD 2022]. Commercial entrepreneurial activities, single or joined in markets, have social implications and can strengthen community bonds in reconstruction processes [HAEFFELE AND CRAIG 2020].

g. **PRODUCTIVE SPACES:** Reconnecting productive chains and city-making can play a significant role in controlling urban metamorphosis. Light industrial plants can be placed temporarily in key areas of the city, used to significantly shorten reconstruction processes while maximizing local content and, in the longer term, be adapted to different uses. Agricultural productions can be inserted organically in the urban pattern and used to set limits to urban growth.

h. **UPGRADING:** Existing nonhistorical patterns can be damaged but not fully destroyed and require mechanisms that allow qualitative and quantitative amelioration. Upgrading [SKINNER ET AL. 2004] can deeply alter the existing structures in terms of type, function, and features, and must always be considered in a larger framework of intervention, shifting the focus from single elements to a processual vision.

Urban triggers can intercept and mix the above-mentioned categories, the fundamental element being the sensible design attitude that allows their adaptive and progressive definition and fruitful application. The quest for the control of urban metamorphosis leads to a state of dynamic equilibrium to be controlled and continuously renegotiated with community needs and aspirations in mind.

6_DESIGN

URBAN TRIGGERS: BACKBONES

●

STREETS
AND PATHS

←

Public intervention reshaping streets in terms of size and nature can initiate a complete rethinking of the visual and user relationship in terms of density and diversity.

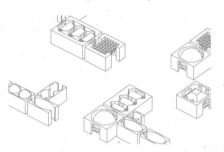

CONSTRUCTION
TECHNIQUES

←

Construction choices suitable to the respective economic, social, and cultural conditions can set the pace for the modification of the urban form.

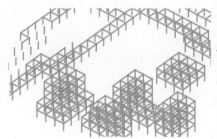

PLOTS
AND PROPERTIES

←

The range of decisions from total maintenance of the grid to complete redrawing of the plots foresees an infinite number of urban models.

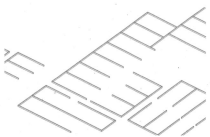

6_ DESIGN

SERVICES

←

Issues such as water accessibility, sanitation, and energy can become precious drivers to attract or reduce density in specific parts of the urban pattern.

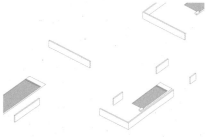

6_ DESIGN

LEVEL OF PRIVACY

←

Empty spaces enrich urban patterns and act as mediation spaces between private and public areas providing different levels of privacy suitable to different uses.

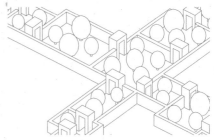

COMMERCIAL AREAS

←

Dislocated commercial activities that are inserted organically in the urban environment can substantially increase the level of proximity and strengthen community bonds.

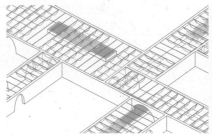

PRODUCTIVE
SPACES

←

Reconnecting productive chains and city-making can play a significant role in controlling urban metamorphosis, thus maximizing the local content.

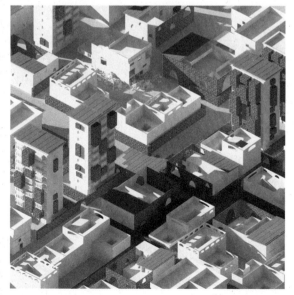

UPGRADING

←

Existing nonhistorical patterns can be damaged but not fully destroyed and require mechanisms that allow qualitative and quantitative amelioration.

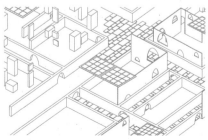

6_4   **INDUCED DESIGN**

Once the public backbone has been defined, regardless of its level of complexity and design sophistication, the urban triggers design approach can evolve in a successful way only if the reactions to the public intervention are coordinated and controlled. The average level of technical knowledge and spatial awareness of the general public in most parts of the world, even in those places where self-construction remains the main building process, is insufficient to allow a spontaneous reaction to the public backbone. The traditional construction methods and building processes, which significantly limited possibilities, allowed historical cities to grow coherently with respect to social, climatic, and economic specificities in accordance with available resources, while widespread access to urban models globally has paradoxically homogenized and oversimplified city-making processes [LEMOINE-RODRÍGUEZ ET AL. 2020], thus transforming some devices into "mantras" [D'ALFONSO AND GALLI 2018] to be uncritically repeated.

Cities can be shaped in a way that adheres to the true needs of the local population only if a process of induced design is devised and applied. Design choices should not be forced on local communities, but rather defined jointly, through the use of laboratories of reconstruction, establishing spatial literacy as an element of general education, just like alphabetization [BENEVOLO 1976]. It is fundamental to keep in mind that the asymmetry in the level of knowledge between professional experts and the general public should not be seen as an unavoidable destiny, but as a necessary evil to be always accepted with skepticism [ILLICH ET AL. 1977]. Induced design mechanisms in relationship to the negotiated backbones can be defined through four main categories of intervention, which can be weaved and overlapped:

a.	**STREETS AND PATHS:**	Architecture without architects [RUDOFSKY 1964] has always represented a vast majority of global constructions, and the possibility of extending local practices to face contemporary challenges has often been explored. Self-construction tools can be applied through processes of guidance that ensure quality and can also control the range of variations, while inserting construction into a wider production chain, thus ensuring a balance between formal institutionalization and complete spontaneism. Self-build is a powerful tool for economic development: the first step in knowledge recovery that can eventually lead to the establishment of numerous small-scale companies playing an active role in urban reconstruction.
b.	**DESIGN MANUALS:**	The drafting of an organized set of prescriptions [GALLI 2019], adapted to the specific needs of each location, can provide the local community with the complete extent of possibilities

in terms of architectural types and physical features, as well as materials and technologies. The design toolbox provides design experts with quantitative parameters and qualitative advice that must be interpreted and included in their own creative process in an anti-deterministic vision that permits maximum variability.

c. **STRUCTURAL TECHNOLOGIES:** The unification of the technological decisions, particularly those regarding structural elements and their pace (FANELLI AND GARGIANI 2002), allows one to foresee a general skeleton of the whole urban cell to be filled and modified according to single households and community needs. Technologies need to be selected in order to ensure a high level of flexibility and customization, while the establishment of light productive plants on site can substantially increase local economic development.

d. **DESIGNERS POOL:** Local architects can be organized in groups that abandon authorial claims in favor of a collective intelligence experiment where the different buildings to be constructed are designed in a collaborative way following a shared and agreed set of basic principles. Design can become a shared action between different professionals who split resources, effort, and fees so as to allow a consistent increase in the average level of quality and to grow the civic value of the category.

6_ DESIGN

The public backbone triggers the pairing of private spaces in a process that tends to induct positive design decisions, maximizing urban quality and minimizing the waste of natural, economic, and social resources. Through the use of urban triggers and mechanisms, cities become generative systems, with public spaces acting as regulatory elements of the overall urban morphologies. This design approach defines a completely different time frame for design action, which, rather than being a process carried out in a specific period and leading to a set result, becomes a system of continuous care and control of urban metamorphosis.

URBAN TRIGGERS: INDUCED DESIGN

•

SELF-BUILD
←

Self-construction can be carried out with processes of guidance that ensure quality, control the range of variations, and guarantee a balance between institutionalization and spontaneism.

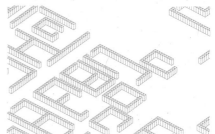

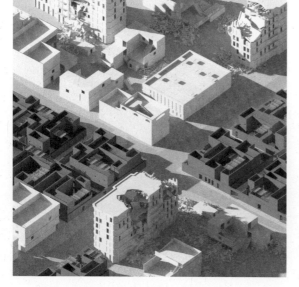

DESIGN MANUALS
←

The drafting of an organized set of prescriptions can provide the local community with the complete range of possibilities (types, features, materials, technologies, etc.).

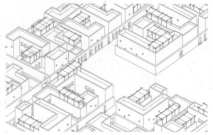

STRUCTURAL TECHNOLOGIES

←

The unification of structural elements allows one to foresee a general skeleton of the city to be filled and modified according to single households and community needs.

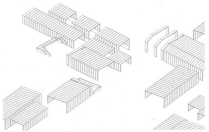

6_ DESIGN

DESIGNERS' POOL

←

Local architects can be organized in groups that abandon authorial claims in favor of a collaborative design process following a shared and agreed set of basic principles.

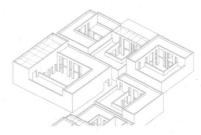

6_5 GROWING EVOLUTIONARY MECHANISMS

The design process in the urban triggers vision becomes the progressive definition of the deep character of the urban fabric, the identification and construction of devices capable of defining the urban framework, and the continuous control of the multitude of responses in the long time frame. It is a vision that abandons any kind of traced and obligatory path to instead fully embrace the uncertainties of an evolutionary process of growth, where open rules are set and can potentially be continuously updated and perfected, though the final results are not immediately predictable. It is an urban design mechanism that escapes any authorial and egotistic will, but does not in any way abandon the creative and unexpected contribution of the individual designer. Two types of radically innovative design operations are defined: on the one hand, the description and spatial configuration of the desired characteristics of the urban fabric and of the triggers, intended both as urban elements and as reference parameters; and on the other hand, the response systems that rely on the creativity of each individual designer, channeled in a coherent process that moves in a variable but defined range. It is not a heterodirected, deterministic process in which everything is decided beforehand, nor a deaf demand for futile creative freedom, but rather the transformation of the design process into an assumption of responsibility toward local communities, available resources, and future generations.

The growing evolutionary mechanism defined by urban triggers can generate a finite but still very large quantity of spatial configurations at the urban scale, and in general returns a dynamic state potentially subject to constant change. It is possible to establish systems of control and forecast of urban metamorphosis through algorithms that parameterize the design choices in the form of mathematical expression, systems that can generate the full range of different spatial configurations. The algorithms can be modified at any time, as the relevant external parameters vary and can be continuously readjusted to the pressures that characterize each site of application. The use of simulations coming from the mathematical modeling of biological systems such as birth-and-death growth models (ALLEN 2007; BATTY 2013; ROSSI ET AL. 2019) allows one to generate virtual cities and compare them to best practices such as historic urban patterns, which can be considered as benchmarks for high-quality solutions. The fine tuning and optimization of the algorithm (ROSSI ET AL. 2014) fosters an understanding of the optimal features of the public backbone, their ideal placement within the urban pattern, and the system of hooking private spaces through induced design, while the clear definition of a set of spatial parameters will significantly limit the volatility of the results.

Only through a new design approach does it become possible to imagine reconstructed cities from a perspective of true transition toward an urban structure capable of responding to the pressures caused by the global risk society paradigm. It is a radical but necessary hypothesis, given the demonstrated inability of current design systems to deal with the complexities of the contemporary world and their prefigurable increase in the near future. It is a profound and systemic change that involves multiple levels: administrative systems, professional practice, urban planning regulations, production, and transformation processes. But it is, above all, a deep change in attitude within a vision that painstakingly tries to reconnect society and urban spaces in order to return an alternative model to the future. The change will not be immediate and complete, but it will necessarily have to pass through courageous attempts, leaps forward, and inevitable failures. *Cities Under Pressure* traces a path: the point of arrival is dark, but the first lights can be seen in the distance and the road is mapped, so all that remains is to gather the courage to begin the journey.

6_ DESIGN

PATTERNS OF GROWING
EVOLUTIONARY MECHANISMS
→

The public backbone is a complete reshaping of public space, which redefines mobility and commercial areas by adjoining the model of the Arab souk to the contemporary urban needs of mixed-use, nonprogrammatic spaces. The induced design of private housing blocks assumes traditional courtyard houses as a reference system that can be redesigned to maximize living density. Starting from these few recurring elements, the range of evolution and metamorphosis of the urban form can be simulated and controlled.

BACKBONES

Street

Commercial

INDUCED DESIGN

Private spaces

 Single-floor module + courtyard

 Multi-floor module + courtyard

Public spaces

 Public building

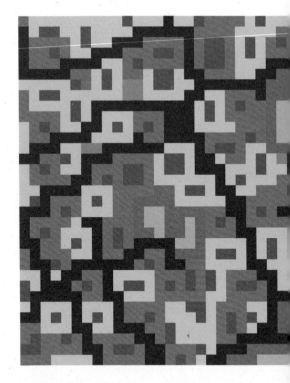

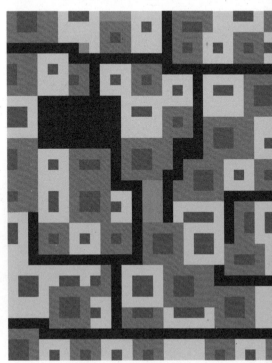

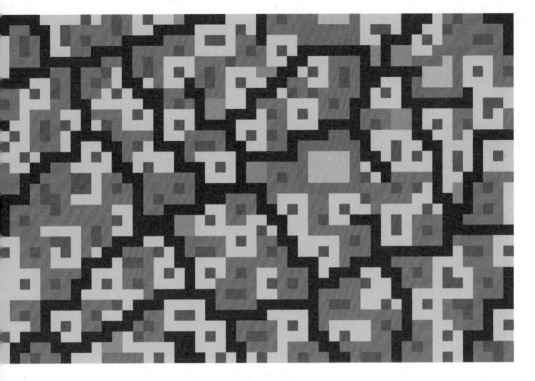

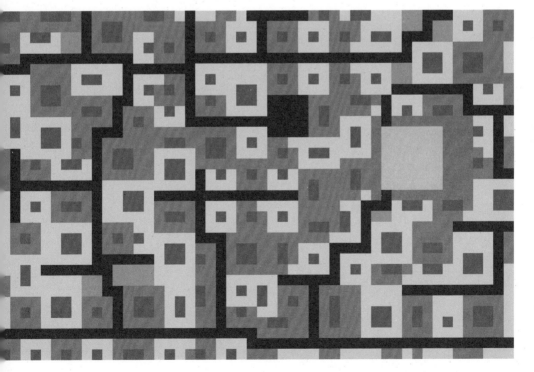

6_ DESIGN

BIBLIOGRAPHY

●

Introduction

Dioum, Baba. "Lecture." General Assembly of the International Union for the Conservation of Nature. New Delhi, 1968.

1.   **GLOBAL CHALLENGES**

1.1   **The City in the Risk Society**

Beck, Ulrich. "The Terrorist Threat: World Risk Society Revisited." *Theory, Culture and Society* 19 (2002), 17–44.

Giannuzzi, Mariaenrica. "Anthropop: Filosofie non tristi per pensare il cambiamento climatico." *Effimera* (2017).

Klein, Naomi. *This Changes Everything: Capitalism vs. the Climate*. New York: Simon & Schuster, 2014.

Leonardi, Emanuele, and Alessandro Barbero. "Il Sintomo Antropocene." Introduction to Jason W. Moore, *Antropocene o Capitalocene? Scenari di ecologia-mondo nell'era della crisi planetaria*, 7–26. Verona: Ombre Corte, 2017.

Žižek, Slavoj. *Living in the End Times*. London: Verso, 2011.

1.2   **Urbicide and Violence**

Bacevich, Andrew. "Social Work with Guns." *London Review of Books* 13, no. 24 (2009), 7–8.

Bogdanovic, Bogdan. "Murder of the City." *The New York Review* 40, no. 10 (1993), 20.

Caro, Robert. *The Power Broker: Robert Moses and the Fall of New York*. New York: Knopf, 1974.

De Carlo, Giancarlo. "Per Mostar." *Spazio e Società* 77 (January–March 1997), 6–9.

Graham, Stephen. *Cities Under Siege: The New Military Urbanism*. London: Verso, 2010, 85–86.

Hippler, Thomas. *Governing from the Sky: A Global History of Aerial Bombing*. London: Verso, 2014.

Hossein-Zadeh, Ismael. *The Political Economy of U.S. Militarism*. New York: Palgrave Macmillan, 2006.

Ribarevic-Nikolic, Ivanka, and Zeljko Juric, eds. *Mostar '92 – Urbicid* (Mostar: Hrvatsko vijece obrane opcine Mostar, 1992).

Sewall, Sarah. Introduction to *The U.S. Army/ Marine Corps Counterinsurgency Field Manual* (Chicago: University of Chicago Press, 2007).

Shaw, Martin. "New Wars of the City: Relationships of 'Urbicide' and 'Genocide'." In *Cities, War, and Terrorism: Towards an Urban Geopolitics*, edited by Stephen Graham, 141–53. Oxford and Cambridge, MA: Blackwell Publishing, 2005.

Smith, Rupert. *The Utility of Force: The Art of War in the Modern World*. London: Allen Lane, 2005.

1.3   **Conflict Recurrence**

Ismail, Salwa. *The Rule of Violence: Subjectivity, Memory and Government in Syria*. Cambridge: Cambridge University Press, 2018.

Mbembe, Achille. "Necropolitics." *Public Culture Winter* 15, no. 1 (2003), 11–40.

World Bank. *World Development Report: Conflict, Security and Development*. Washington, DC: World Bank, 2011.

BIBLIOGRAPHY

————. *The Toll of War: The Economic and Social Consequences of the Conflict in Syria*. Washington, DC: World Bank, 2017.

————. *Building Peace: Reconstruction for Security, Sustainable Peace and Equity in MENA*. Washington, DC: World Bank, 2020, 9.

1.4   **Disasters and Climate Change**

Aquilué Jungend, Inés. *Ciudad e Incertidumbre*. Barcelona: Ediciones Asimétricas, 2021.

Avallone, Gennaro. "Il grande balzo del 'capitalocene' sulla natura." *Il Manifesto* (July 7, 2017).

Bertin, Mattia, Francesco Musco, and Lorenzo Fabian. "Rethinking Planning Hierarchy Considering Climate Change as Global Catastrophe." *Climate Risk Management* 30 (2020).

Birkmann, Joern, and Korinna von Teichman. "Integrating Disaster Risk Reduction and Climate Change Adaptation: Key Challenges—Scales, Knowledge, and Norms." *Sustainability Science* 5, no. 2 (2010), 171–84.

Crutzen, Paul. "The Anthropocene." In *Earth System Science in the Anthropocene*, edited by Eckart Ehlers and Thomas Krafft. Berlin and Heidelberg: Springer, 2006.

Forino, Giuseppe, Jason von Meding, and Graham Brewer. "A Conceptual Governance Framework for Climate Change Adaptation and Disaster Risk Reduction Integration." *International Journal of Disaster Risk Science* 6, no. 4 (2015), 372–84.

Gallopin, Gilberto. "Linkages between Vulnerability, Resilience, and Adaptive Capacity." *Global Environmental Change* 16, no. 3 (2006), 293–303.

Isenhour, Cindy, Gary McDonogh, and Melissa Checker. *Sustainability in the Global City: Myth and Practice*. New York: Cambridge University Press, 2015.

Klein, Naomi. *This Changes Everything: Capitalism vs. the Climate*. New York: Simon & Schuster, 2014.

McNeill, John, and Peter Engelke. The *Great Acceleration: An Environmental History of the Anthropocene since 1945*. Cambridge, MA: Harvard University Press, 2014.

Moore, Jason. *Anthropocene or Capitalocene?: Nature, History, and the Crisis of Capitalism*. Oakland: PM Press, 2016.

Ramroth, William. *Planning for Disaster: How Natural and Man-Made Disasters Shape the Built Environment*. New York: Kaplan Publisher, 2007.

Robinson, Mary. *Climate Justice: Hope, Resilience and the Fight for a Sustainable Future*. London: Bloomsbury Publishing, 2018.

Sanderson, David, Jerold Kayden, and Julia Leis, eds. *Urban Disaster Resilience: New Dimensions from International Practice in the Built Environment*. New York: Routledge, 2016.

1.5   **Social and Economic Risks**

Agier, Michel. *Managing the Undesirables: Refugee Camps and Humanitarian Government*. Cambridge: Polity Press, 2011.

Bagaeen, Samer, and Ola Uduku. *Gated Communities: Social Sustainability in Contemporary and Historical Gated Developments*. London: Taylor and Francis, 2012.

Banerjee, Abhijit, and Esther Duflo. *Poor Economics: A Radical Rethinking of the Way to Fight Global Poverty*. New York: PublicAffairs, 2011.

Blakeley, Grace. *The Corona Crash: How the Pandemic Will Change Capitalism*. London: Verso, 2020.

Brundtland, Gro Harlem. *Our Common Future*. Oxford: Oxford University Press, 1987.

Consigliere, Stefania, and Cristina Zavaroni. "Come siamo arrivati fin qui? Il contagio di un'idea di salute." *Giap* (December 7, 2020).

Davis, Mike. *Planet of Slums*. London: Verso, 2005.

De Angelis, Massimo. *Omnia Sunt Communia: On the Commons and the Transformation to Postcapitalism*. London: Zed Books, 2017.

Harvey, David. *Rebel Cities: From the Right to the City to the Urban Revolution*. London: Verso, 2012.

Hess, Charlotte, and Elinor Ostrom. *Understanding Knowledge as a Commons: From Theory to*

BIBLIOGRAPHY

Practice. Cambridge, MA: MIT Press, 2007.

Kripa, Ersela, and Stephen Mueller. *Fronts: Military Urbanisms and the Developing World.* New York: Applied Research + Design Publishing, 2020.

Milanović, Branko. *Global Inequality: A New Approach for the Age of Globalization.* Cambridge, MA: Harvard University Press, 2016.

Mostafavi, Mohsen. *Ethics of the Urban: The City and the Spaces of the Political.* Zurich: Lars Müller Publishers, 2017.

Ostrom, Elinor. *Governing the Commons: The Evolution of Institutions for Collective Action.* Cambridge: Cambridge University Press, 1990.

Putnam, Robert D. *Bowling Alone: The Collapse and Revival of American Community.* New York: Simon & Schuster, 2000.

Rabbat, Nasser. "The Arab Revolution Takes Back the Public Space." *Critical Inquiry* 39, no. 1 (2012), 198–208.

Secchi, Bernardo. *La città dei ricchi e la città dei poveri.* Rome and Bari: Laterza, 2013.

Stein, Samuel. *Capital City: Gentrification and the Real Estate State.* London: Verso, 2019.

Zetter, Roger, and Camillo Boano. "Making Space and Place after Natural Disasters and Forced Displacement." In *Post Disaster Reconstruction: From Emergency to Sustainability*, edited by Gonzalo Lizarralde, Cassidy Johnson, and Colin Davidson. London: Taylor and Francis, 2010.

2. HISTORICAL EXPÉRIENCES

2.1 Reassessing Reconstruction

Allais, Lucia. *Designs of Destruction: The Making of Monuments in the Twentieth Century.* Chicago: University of Chicago Press, 2018, 2.

Bevan, Robert. *The Destruction of Memory: Architecture at War.* Chicago: University of Chicago Press, 2006.

Bold, John, Peter Larkham, and Robert Pickard, eds. *Authentic Reconstruction: Authenticity, Architecture and the Built Heritage.* London: Bloomsbury, 2017.

Cogato-Lanza, Elena, and Patrizia Bonifazio. *Les experts de la reconstruction: Gli Esperti della ricostruzione.* Geneva: Metis Presses, 2009.

Cohen, Jean-Louis. *Architecture in Uniform: Design and Building for the Second World War.* Montreal: Canadian Centre for Architecture, 2011.

Coward, Martin. *Urbicide: The Politics of Urban Destruction.* London: Routledge, 2004.

Diefendorf, Jeffry, ed. *Rebuilding Europe's Bombed Cities.* New York: Palgrave Macmillan, 1990.

Düwel, Jörn, and Nils Gutschow. *A Blessing in Disguise: War and Town Planning in Europe, 1940–1945.* Berlin: DOM Publishers, 2013.

Franke, Anselm. *Territories: Islands, Camps and Other States of Utopia.* Berlin: KW Institute for Contemporary Art, 2003.

Geddes, Patrick, and Gilbert Slater. *Ideas at War.* London: Williams & Norgate *(The Making of the Future series)*, 1917.

Hippler, Thomas. *Governing from the Sky: A Global History of Aerial Bombing.* London: Verso, 2014.

Iklé, Fred. *Every War Must End.* New York: Columbia University Press, 2005.

Johnson-Marshall, Percy. *Rebuilding Cities: From Medieval to Modern Times.* Livingston, NJ: Transaction Publishers, 2010.

Mamoli, Marcello, and Giorgio Trebbi. *Storia dell'Urbanistica: L'Europa del Secondo Dopoguerra.* Rome and Bari: Laterza, 1988.

Moravánszky, Ákos, ed. *Re-Humanizing Architecture: New Forms of Community, 1950–1970.* Basel: Birkhäuser Verlag, 2016.

Porteous, Douglas, and Sandra Smith. *Domicide: The Global Destruction of Home.* Montreal: McGill-Queen's University Press, 2001.

Shrady, Nicholas. *The Last Day: Wrath, Ruin, and Reason in the Great Lisbon Earthquake of 1755.* London: Penguin, 2009.

Vale, Lawrence, and Thomas Campanella. *The Resilient City: How Modern Cities Recover from Disaster.* Oxford: Oxford University Press, 2005.

Weizman, Eyal. *The Least of All Possible Evils: Humanitarian Violence from Arendt to Gaza.* London: Verso, 2011.

———. *Forensic Architecture: Violence at the Threshold of Detectability.* New York: Zone Books, 2018.

2.2   Transformation Map

Benevolo, Leonardo. *The Origins of Modern Town Planning.* Cambridge, MA: MIT Press, 1971.

———. "Le due tradizioni dell'architettura contemporanea." *Casabella* 544 (1988), 50–53.

———. "La percezione dell'invisibile: Piazza San Pietro del Bernini." *Casabella* 572 (1990), 54–62.

———. *La Cattura dell'Infinito.* Rome and Bari: Laterza, 1991.

———. *San Pietro e la città di Roma.* Rome and Bari: Laterza, 2004.

2.3   Classifying Reconstruction

Brown, Daniel, Stephen Platt, and John Bevington. *Disaster Recovery Indicators: Guidelines for Monitoring and Evaluation.* Cambridge: Cambridge University Centre for Risk in the Built Environment (CURBE), 2010.

Mamoli, Marcello, and Giorgio Trebbi. *Storia dell'Urbanistica: L'Europa del Secondo Dopoguerra.* Rome and Bari: Laterza, 1988.

2.4   Unprecedented Scale of Destruction

Clement, Viviane, Kanta Kumari Rigaud, Alex de Sherbinin, Bryan Jones, Susana Adamo, Jacob Schewe, Nian Sadiq, and Elham Shabahat. *Groundswell Part 2: Acting on Internal Climate Migration.* Washington, DC: World Bank, 2021.

Davis, Mike. "Fear and Money in Dubai." *New Left Review* 41 (2006), 47–68.

Dougherty, Conor. *Golden Gates: The Housing Crisis and a Reckoning for the American Dream.* New York: Penguin Books, 2021.

Elsheshtawy, Yasser. *Dubai: Behind an Urban Spectacle.* London: Routledge, 2009.

Femia, Francesco, and Caitlin Werrell. "Syria: Climate Change, Drought, and Social Unrest." *The Center for Climate and Security* 29 (2012).

Gleick, Peter. "Water, Drought, Climate Change, and Conflict in Syria." *Weather, Climate, and Society* 6, no. 3 (2014), 331–40.

Harris, Marc, Robert Dixon, Nicholas Melin, Daniel Hendrex, Richard Russo, and Michael Bailey. *Megacities and the United States Army: Preparing for a Complex and Uncertain Future.* Washington, DC: Strategic Studies Group, 2014.

Konaev, Margarita. "The Future of Urban Warfare in the Age of Megacities." *Focus stratégique* 88 (2019).

Lyons, Kate. "Why Is Indonesia Moving Its Capital City?" *The Guardian*, August 27, 2019.

Manjoo, Farhad. "It's the End of California as We Know It." *The New York Times*, October 30, 2019.

Mumford, Lewis. *The City in History: Its Origins, Its Transformations, and Its Prospects.* San Diego: Harcourt, Brace and World, 1961, 116.

Nakate, Vanessa. "We Are Facing the Same Storm, but We Are in Different Boats." In *Property Will Cost Us the Earth*, edited by Jessie Kindig. London: Verso, 2022.

Parsons, Adam. "Global Warming: The Great Equaliser." *Share the World's Resources*, September 1, 2007.

Van Loenhout, Joris, and Regina Below. *The Human Cost of Disasters: An Overview of the Last 20 Years (2000–2019).* Geneva: UNDRR, 2019.

Zittis, George, Panos Hadjinicolaou, Mansour Almazroui, Edoardo Bucchignani, Fatima Driouech, Khalid El Rhaz, Levent Kurnaz, Grigory Nikulin, Athanasios Ntoumos, Tugba Ozturk, Yiannis Proestos, Georgiy Stenchikov, Rashyd Zaaboul, and Jos Lelieveld. "Business-as-Usual Will Lead to Super and Ultra-Extreme Heatwaves in the Middle East and North Africa." *Climate and Atmospheric Science* 4, no. 20 (2021).

BIBLIOGRAPHY

3_ **STRATEGY**

3_1 **Top Down / Bottom Up**

Banerjee, Banashree, Claudio Acioly, Axumite Gebre-Egziabher, Joan Clos, and Katja Dietrich. *Streets as Tools for Urban Transformation in Slums: A Street-Led Approach to Citywide Slum Upgrading.* Nairobi: UN Habitat, 2012.

Bartling, Hugh. *Sustainable Suburbia? Rethinking the North American Metropolis.* New York: Taylor & Francis, 2014.

Charlesworth, Esther. *Humanitarian Architecture: 15 Stories of Architects Working After Disaster.* New York: Taylor & Francis, 2014.

Heynen, Hilde. *Architecture and Modernity: A Critique.* Cambridge, MA: MIT Press, 1999.

Schwab, James. *Planning for Post-Disaster Recovery: Next Generation.* Chicago: American Planning Association, 2014.

Sennett, Richard. *The Uses of Disorder: Personal Identity and City Life.* New York: Knopf, 1970.

Sendra, Pablo, and Richard Sennett. *Designing Disorder: Experiments and Disruptions in the City.* London: Verso, 2020.

Skinner, Reinhard, Matthew French, Claudio Acioly, and Jane Reid. *A Practical Guide to Designing, Planning, and Executing Citywide Slum Upgrading Programmes.* Nairobi: UN Habitat, 2015.

Tafuri, Manfredo. *Progetto e Utopia: Architettura e Sviluppo Capitalistico.* Rome and Bari: Laterza, 1973.

United Nations Office for Disaster Risk Reduction. *Sendai Framework for Disaster Risk Reduction 2015–2012.* Geneva: United Nations Office for Disaster Risk Reduction, 2015.

3_2 **Cataclysmic Credit / Gradual Credit**

Armendáriz, Beatriz, and Jonathan Morduch. *The Economics of Microfinance.* Cambridge, MA: MIT Press, 2005.

Bowen, Stuart. *Hard Lessons: The Iraq Reconstruction Experience.* Washington, DC: Special Inspector General for Iraq Reconstruction, 2009.

Grima, Simon, Osman Sirkeci, and Kamuran Elbeyoglu. *Global Street Economy and Micro Entrepreneurship.* Bingley: Emerald Publishing Limited, 2020.

Jacobs, Jane. *The Death and Life of the Great American Cities.* New York: Random House, 1961, 293–94.

Olawuyi, Damilola. *Local Content and Sustainable Development in Global Energy Markets.* Cambridge: Cambridge University Press, 2021.

Robinson, James, and Ragnar Torvik. "White Elephants." *Journal of Public Economics* 89 (2005), 197–210.

Yunus, Muhammad. *Creating a World Without Poverty: Social Business and the Future of Capitalism.* New York: PublicAffairs, 2007.

3_3 **Layers / Cells**

Baker, Lawrence. *The Water Environment of Cities.* New York: Springer, 2009.

Brown, Lester. *Plan B 4.0: Mobilizing to Save Civilization.* New York: Earth Policy Institute, 2009.

Bruegman, Robert. *Sprawl: A Compact History.* Chicago: University of Chicago Press, 2005.

Elcker, Ursula. *Urban Energy Systems for Low-Carbon Cities.* Rotterdam: Elsevier, 2018.

Harris, Richard. "Lawrence A. Herzog: Global Suburbs: Urban Sprawl from the Rio Grande to Rio De Janeiro." *Building & Landscapes* 22, no. 2 (2015).

Junginger, Sabine. *Transforming Public Services by Design: Re-Orienting Policies, Organizations and Services around People.* London: Taylor and Francis, 2016.

Keucheyan, Razmig. *La nature est un champ de bataille: Essai d'écologie politique.* Paris: Éditions de la Découverte, 2014.

Lozano, Eduardo. *Community Design and the Culture of Cities: The Crossroad and the Wall.* Cambridge: Cambridge University Press, 1990.

Marx, Paris. *Road to Nowhere: What Silicon Valley Gets Wrong about the Future of Transportation.* London: Verso, 2022.

BIBLIOGRAPHY

Mumford, Lewis. *The City in History: Its Origins, Its Transformations, and Its Prospects*. San Diego: Harcourt, Brace and World, 1961.

Piacenti, Giulia. "L'idea di unità di quartiere: La ricostruzione della piccola dimensione." PhD diss., Università Iuav di Venezia, 2022.

Rolnik, Raquel. *Urban Warfare: Housing Under the Empire of Finance*. London: Verso, 2016.

3_4 **Project / Process**

Albrecht, Benno, and Leonardo Benevolo. "La questione del centro archeologico di Roma." *Casabella* 569 (1990), 35–37.

Benevolo, Leonardo. *Metamorfosi della città*. Milan: Libri Scheiwiller, 1996.

Boano, Camillo. *Progetto Minore: Alla ricerca della minorità nel progetto urbanistico ed architettonico*. Siracusa: Lettera 22, 2020, 71.

Gregotti, Vittorio. *Il territorio dell'Architettura*. Milan: Feltrinelli, 1966.

Nicolin, Pierluigi, ed. "Progetto debole / The Weak Design." *Lotus International* 62 (1989).

Sale, Kirkpatrick. *Dwellers in the Land: The Bioregional Vision*. San Francisco: Sierra Club Books, 1985.

Vattimo, Gianni, and Pier Aldo Rovatti. *Il Pensiero Debole*. Milan: Feltrinelli, 1983.

3_5 **Reconstruction Laboratory**

Abrams, Charles, and Otto Koenigsberger. *Report on Housing in the Gold Coast*. New York: United Nations Technical Assistance Programme, 1956.

———. *Report on Housing in the Philippine Islands*. New York: United Nations Technical Assistance Programme, 1959.

———. *Growth and Urban Renewal in Singapore*. New York: United Nations Technical Assistance Programme, 1963.

Adler, Emanuel, and Michael Barnett. *Security Communities*. Cambridge: Cambridge University Press, 2014.

Alexander, Christopher. *The Production of Houses*. Oxford: Oxford University Press, 1985.

Blewitt, John. *Understanding Sustainable Development*. London: Routledge, 2018.

Caminos, Horacio. *Interim Urbanization Project Dandora, Nairobi, Kenya: A Progressive Development Proposal, Including a Site and Services Model*. Cambridge, MA: Massachusetts Institute of Technology, 1973.

Crane, Jacob Leslie. *La vivienda obrera en Puerto Rico*. Puerto Rico: Oficina Internacional del Trabajo, 1944.

Dini, Massimo. *Renzo Piano: Projects and Buildings, 1964–1983*. Milan: Electa, 1984.

Doshi, Balkrishna. *Balkrishna Doshi: Architecture for the People*. Basel: Vitra Design Museum, 2019.

Habraken, Nicolaas John. *Supports: An Alternative to Mass Housing*. London: Routledge, 1999.

Ismail, Aquila. *The Story of Khuda ki basti: Shelter for the Shelterless*. Karachi: City Press, 2002.

Machado, Rodolfo. *The Favela-Bairro Project: Jorge Mario Jauregui Architects*. Cambridge, MA: Harvard Graduate School of Design, 2003.

Pappalardo, Serena. "Le Origini del Progressive Development Approach: I paradigmi di una progettazione incrementale." PhD diss., Università Iuav di Venezia, 2021.

Turner, John. *Housing by People: Towards Autonomy in Building Environments*. London: Marion Boyars Books, 1976.

World Bank. *Building Peace: Reconstruction for Security, Sustainable Peace and Equity in MENA*. Washington, DC: World Bank, 2020.

3_6 **Operational Phases**

Aldrich, Daniel P. "Ties that Bond, Ties that Build: Social Capital and Governments in Post Disaster Recovery." *Studies in Emergent Order* 4 (2011), 58–68.

Environmental Protection Agency (EPA). *America's Water Infrastructure Act: Risk Assessments and Emergency Response Plans*. Washington, DC: EPA, 2018.

Federal Emergency Management Agency (FEMA). *Four Phases of Emergency Management*. Washington, DC: FEMA, 2020.

Ireni-Saban, Liza. "Challenging Disaster Administration: Toward Community-Based Disaster Resilience." *Administration & Society* 45, no. 6 (2012), 651–73.

United Nations General Assembly (UNGA). *Report of the Open-Ended Intergovernmental Expert 2 Working Group on Indicators and Terminology Relating to Disaster Risk Reduction*. New York: UN, 2016, 11.

United Nations. *Joint Recovery and Peacebuilding Assessments (RPBAs): A Practical Note to Assessment and Planning*. New York: UN, 2008.

United Nations Office for Disaster Risk Reduction (UNDRR). *Yokohama Strategy and Plan of Action for a Safer World: Guidelines to Natural Disaster Prevention, Preparedness and Mitigation*. Geneva: UNDRR, 1994.

———. *Sendai Framework for Disaster Risk Reduction 2015–2030*. Geneva: UNDRR, 2015.

———. *UN Global Assessment Report on Disaster Risk Reduction (GAR)*. Geneva: UNDRR, 2019.

Vaughn, John. "Community Development in a Post-Conflict Context: Fracture and Depleted Social Capital." *Community Development Journal* 46, no. 1 (2011), 51–65.

4_ **SUSTAINABLE TRANSITION**

4_1 **Exporting the Historical Core**

Albrecht, Benno, and Anna Magrin. *Esportare il Centro Storico*. Rimini: Guaraldi, 2015.

Benevolo, Leonardo. *La città e l'architetto*. Rome and Bari: Laterza, 1984, 92.

———. *The European City*. Oxford and Cambridge, MA: Blackwell, 1993, 215.

Braudel, Fernand. *Storia, misura del mondo*. Bologna: Il Mulino, 1998.

Halegoua, Germaine. *Smart Cities*. Cambridge, MA: MIT Press, 2020.

Harvey, David. *Rebel Cities: From the Right to the City to the Urban Revolution*. London: Verso, 2012, 4.

Lefebvre, Henri. *Le droit a la ville*. Paris: Anthropos, 1968.

Marino, Marco. "Il progetto della città medievale: Indagine sulla crescita di San Gimignano." PhD diss., Università Iuav di Venezia, 2021.

Morozov, Evgeny, and Francesca Bria. *Ripensare la smart city*. Turin: Codice Edizioni, 2018, 76.

Muratori, Saverio. *Studi per una operante storia urbana di Venezia*. Rome: Istituto Poligrafico dello Stato, 1960.

Raco, Mike, and Federico Savini. *Planning and Knowledge: How New Forms of Technocracy Are Shaping Contemporary Cities*. Bristol: Policy Press, 2019.

Yamagata, Yoshiki, and Perry Yang. *Urban Systems Design: Creating Sustainable Smart Cities in the Internet of Things*. Amsterdam: Elsevier, 2020.

4_2 **The Leap Forward**

Archibugi, Daniele, and Carlo Pietrobelli. "The Globalisation of Technology and Its Implications for Developing Countries: Windows of Opportunity or Further Burden?" *Technological Forecasting and Social Change* 70 (2003), 861–83.

Asimakopoulou, Eleana, and Nik Bessis. *Advanced ICTs for Disaster Management and Threat Detection: Collaborative and Distributed Framework*. New York: Information Science Reference, 2010.

Bailard, Catie Snow. "Ethnic Conflict Goes Mobile: Mobile Technology's Effect on the Opportunities and Motivations for Violent Collective Action." *Journal of Peace Research* 52 (2015), 323–37.

Bookchin, Murray. *Remaking Society*. Montreal: Black Rose Books, 1989.

De Angelis, Massimo. *Omnia Sunt Communia: On the Commons and the Transformation to Postcapitalism*. London: Zed Books, 2017.

Fourie, Pieter, Peraphan Jittrapirom, Robert Binder, Michael Tobey, Sergio Ordonez Medina, Tanvi Maheshwari, and Yoshiki Yamagata. *Modeling and Design of Smart Mobility Systems*. Amsterdam: Elsevier, 2020.

Headrick, Daniel. *The Tentacles of Progress: Technology Transfer in the Age of Imperialism, 1850–1940*. Oxford: Oxford University Press, 1988.

Hensher, David, Corinne Mulley, Chinh Ho, Yale Wong, Göran Smith, and John Nelson. *Understanding Mobility as a Service (MaaS): Past, Present and Future*. Dordrecht and New York: Springer, 2020.

Izumi, Takako, and Rajib Shaw, eds. *Disaster Management and Private Sectors: Challenges and Potentials*. Tokyo: Springer Japan, 2015.

Mancini, Francesco. *New Technology and the Prevention of Violence and Conflict*. New York: International Peace Institute, 2013.

Mathews, Race. *Jobs of Our Own: Building a Stakeholder Society; Alternatives to the Market and the State*. London: Pluto Press, 1999.

Moss, Stephen. "End of the Car Age: How Cities Are Outgrowing the Automobile." *The Guardian*, April 28, 2015.

Ostrom, Elinor. *Governing the Commons: The Evolution of Institutions for Collective Action*. Cambridge: Cambridge University Press, 1990.

Pierskalla, Jan, and Florian Hollenbach. "Technology and Collective Action: The Effect of Cell Phone Coverage on Political Violence in Africa." *The American Political Science Review* 107, no. 2 (2013), 207–24.

Poblet, Marta. *Mobile Technologies for Conflict Management: Online Dispute Resolution, Governance, Participation*. Dordrecht and New York: Springer, 2011.

Ramsbotham, Oliver, Hugh Miall, and Tom Woodhouse. *Contemporary Conflict Resolution*. Cambridge: Polity Press, 2011.

Srnicek, Nick, and Alex Williams. *Inventing the Future: Postcapitalism and a World Without Work*. London: Verso, 2015.

———. "#Accelerate: Manifesto for an Accelerationist Politics." In *Accelerate: The Accelerationist Reader*. Edited by Robin Mackay and Armen Avanessian. Berlin: Mervin Verlag, 2014, 356.

United Nations Commission on Science and Technology for Development (UNCTAD). *Bridging the Technology Gap between and within Nations*. Geneva: United Nations, 2006.

4.3 **Decentralized Model**

Archibugi, Daniele. *The Global Commonwealth of Citizens: Toward Cosmopolitan Democracy*. Princeton, NJ: Princeton University Press, 2009.

Bookchin, Murray. "Libertarian Municipalism: An Overview." *Green Perspectives* 24 (1991).

Castoriadis, Cornelius. *La Rivoluzione Democratica: Teoria e progetto dell'autogoverno*. Milan: Eluthera, 2001.

Dahl, Robert. *Democracy and Its Critics*. New Haven, CT: Yale University Press, 1990.

Frey, Bruno. "Direct Democracy: Politico-Economic Lessons from Swiss Experience." *American Economic Review* 84, no. 2 (1994), 338–42.

Frey, Bruno, and Reiner Eichenberger. "FOCJ: Competitive Governments for Europe." *International Review of Law and Economics* 16, no. 3 (1996), 315–27.

———. *The New Democratic Federalism of Europe: Functional, Overlapping and Competing Jurisdiction*. Cheltenham: Edward Elgar, 1999.

Habermas, Jürgen. *The Inclusion of the Other: Studies in Political Theory*. Cambridge, MA: MIT Press, 1998.

Held, David, and Anthony McGrew, eds. *Governing Globalization: Power, Authority, and Global Governance*. Cambridge: Polity Press, 2002.

Khanna, Parag. *Connectography: Mapping the Future of Global Civilization*. New York: Random House, 2016.

Magnaghi, Alberto. *Il progetto locale: Verso la coscienza di luogo*. Turin: Bollati Boringhieri, 2010, 74–75.

4.4 **Adaptive Circularity**

Ellram, Lisa, Lydia Bals, and Wendy Tate, eds. *Circular Economy Supply Chains: From Chains to Systems*. Bingley: Emerald Publishing Limited, 2022.

Magnaghi, Alberto. *Il progetto locale: Verso la coscienza di luogo*. Turin: Bollati Boringhieri, 2010.

Putnam, Robert. *Bowling Alone: The Collapse and Revival of American Community*. New York: Touchstone and Simon & Schuster, 2000.

Sachs, Ignacy. "Environment and Styles of Development." *Economic and Political Weekly* 9, no. 21 (1974), 828–37.

Schumacher, Ernst Friedrich. *Small Is Beautiful: A Study of Economics as if People Mattered*. London: Blond & Briggs, 1973.

5_   EXPLORATIONS

5_1   Settlement Principle as a Chance for Urban Metamorphosis

Benevolo, Leonardo. "Appropriate Habitat." In *Towards a Quality of Life: The Role of Industrialization in the Architecture and Urban Planning of Developing Countries*; Report of the Proceedings of the Second International Congress of Architects, Persepolis, Iran, 1974, edited by Laleh Bakhtiar, 249–50. Teheran: Ministry of Housing and Urban Development, 1976.

5_5   From Hazard to Opportunity: The Controlled Flooding Strategy

Held, Isaac, and Brian Soden. "Robust Responses of the Hydrological Cycle to Global Warming." *Journal of Climate* 19 (2006), 5686–99.

5_7   Piecemeal Planning at Work

Gombrich, Ernst. "The Beauty of Old Towns." *Architectural Association Journal* 80 (1965), 293–97.

6_   DESIGN

6_1   Urban Restoration

Albrecht, Benno, and Anna Magrin. *Esportare il Centro Storico*. Rimini: Guaraldi, 2015.

Bandarin, Francesco, and Ron van Oers. *The Historic Urban Landscape: Managing Heritage in an Urban Century*. Hoboken, NJ: John Wiley & Sons, 2012.

Benevolo, Leonardo. *L'architettura nell'Italia contemporanea: ovvero il tramonto del paesaggio*. Rome and Bari: Laterza, 2006, 188.

Cederna, Antonio. "Salvaguardia dei Centri Storici e Sviluppo Urbanistico." *Casabella* 250 (1961), 48–55.

Cervellati, Pier Luigi, Roberto Scanavini, and Carlo De Angelis. *La nuova cultura delle città: la salvaguardia dei centri storici, la riappropriazione sociale degli organismi urbani e l'analisi dello sviluppo territoriale nell'esperienza di Bologna*. Milan: Mondadori, 1977.

Choay, Françoise. *L'allégorie du patrimoine*. Paris: Seuil, 1992.

Council of Europe. *European Charter of the Architectural Heritage*. Amsterdam: Congress on the European Architectural Heritage, 1975.

6_2   Urban Triggers

Alexander, Christopher. *Notes on the Synthesis of Form*. Cambridge, MA: Harvard University Press, 1964.

Gombrich, Ernst. *Reflections on the History of Art*. Oxford: Phaidon, 1987, 201.

Fry, Edwin Maxwell, and Jane Drew. *Tropical Architecture in the Dry and Humid Zones*. London: Batsford, 1964.

Popper, Karl. *The Poverty of Historicism*. London: Routledge & Kegan Paul, 1957, 66–67.

6_3   Backbones

Banerjee, Banashree, Claudio Acioly, Axumite Gebre-Egziabher, Joan Clos, and Katja Dietrich. *Streets as Tools for Urban Transformation in Slums: A Street-Led Approach to Citywide Slum Upgrading*. Nairobi: UN Habitat, 2012.

Bernoulli, Hans. *Die Stadt und Ihr Boden*. Zurich: Verlag für Architektur, 1946.

Haeffele, Stefanie, and Alexander Wade Craig. "Commercial Social Spaces in the Post-Disaster Context." *Journal of Entrepreneurship and Public Policy* 9, no. 3 (2020), 303–17.

Hallaj, Abdulaziz. "Syrian Cities and the

Challenges of Reconstruction." *In Syria—The Making of the Future: From Urbicide to the Architecture of the City*, edited by Jacopo Galli, 71–97. Venice: Incipit Editore, 2018.

Kanigel, Robert. *Eyes on the Street: The Life of Jane Jacobs.* New York: Random House, 2016.

Narne, Edoardo, and Angelo Bertolazzi. *Abitare intorno a un vuoto: Le residenze a patio dalle origini al contemporaneo.* Venice: Marsilio, 2012.

Skinner, Reinhard, Matthew French, Claudio Acioly, and Jane Reid. *A Practical Guide to Designing, Planning, and Executing Citywide Slum Upgrading Programmes.* Nairobi: UN Habitat, 2015.

Torre, André, and Delphine Gallaud, eds. *Handbook of Proximity Relations.* Cheltenham: Edward Elgar, 2022.

6_4 Induced Design

Benevolo, Leonardo. *La Casa dell'Uomo.* Rome and Bari: Laterza, 1976.

d'Alfonso, Maddalena, and Jacopo Galli. "The Mantra of Modernity." In *Sustainable Urban Development and Globalization: New Strategies for New Challenges—with a Focus on the Global South*, edited by Agostino Petrillo and Paola Bellaviti, 209–20. Berlin and Heidelberg: Springer, 2016.

Fanelli, Giovanni, and Roberto Gargiani. *Auguste Perret.* Rome and Bari: Laterza, 2002.

Galli, Jacopo. *Tropical Toolbox: Fry and Drew and the Search for an African Modernity.* Siracusa: Lettera 22, 2019.

Illich, Ivan, John McKnight, Irving Zola, Jonathan Caplan, and Harley Shaiken. *Disabling Professions.* London: Marion Boyars Publishers, 1977.

Lemoine-Rodríguez, Richard, Luis Inostroza, and Harald Zeppa. "The Global Homogenization of Urban Form: An Assessment of 194 Cities across Time." *Landscape and Urban Planning* 204 (2020).

Rudofsky, Bernard. *Architecture Without Architects: An Introduction to Non-Pedigreed Architecture.* New York: MoMA, 1964.

6_5 Growing Evolutionary Mechanisms

Allen, Linda. *An Introduction to Mathematical Biology.* Upper Saddle River, NJ: Pearson Prentice Hall, 2007.

Batty, Michael. *The New Science of Cities.* Cambridge, MA: MIT Press, 2013.

Rossi, Francesco, Massimo Fornasier, and Benedetto Piccoli. "Mean-Field Sparse Optimal Control." *Phil. Trans. R. Soc.* 372 (2014).

Rossi, Francesco, Giacomo Albi, Mattia Bongini, and Francesco Solombrino. "Leader Formation with Mean-Field Birth and Death Models." *M3AS: Math. Models Meth. Appl. Sc.* 29 (2019), 633–79.

CREDITS

●

CREDITS

INTRODUCTION
Gostomel highway, 3/06/2022, photo by Irpin Municipality, Harasta, Damascus, 26/10/2022, photo by Jacopo Galli. Iskenderun, 9/02/2023, photo by Valerio Nicolosi.

1. GLOBAL CHALLENGES
• Urbicide 1936–2023
Drawing by Andrea Fantin, Urbicide Task Force.
Sources:
Afghanistan: https://population stat.com/ (accessed 01/2023).
Austria: Bevölkerung von Wien 1590–2014 - mit Aktualisierung bis Q4 2016. Eigenes Werk, Statistischen Mitteilungen der Stadt Wien (Heft 4/2000) Statistik Austria. Statistisches Jahrbuch 2009. https://de.wikipedia.org/wiki/Wien#/media/Datei:Population_of_Vienna.svg
Bosnia and Herzegovina: Državni zavod za statistiku Republike Bosne i Hercegovine. "Nacionalni sastav stanovnistva. Nacionalni sastav stanovništva. Rezultati za republiku po opštinama i naseljenim mjestima 1991."

Statistički Bilten no. 234 (1993), 7-76. https://fzs.ba/wp-content/uploads/2016/06/nacionalni-sastav-stanovnistva-po-naseljen im-mjestima-bilten-234.pdf
China: Nanjing: Tokushi cho, Kasahara and Tokushi Kasahara. 南京事件 [The Nanking Incident] Tokyo: Iwanami Shoten, 1997. Shanghai: Henriot Christian Lu Shi and Charlotte Aubrun. *The Population of Shanghai (1865-1953): A Sourcebook.* Leiden: Brill, 2019. https://brill.com/view/title/36402; http://www.chinarhyming.com/2015/06/14/the-1936-shang-hai-census-three-and-a-half-million-folk/
Guangzhou: *Webster's Geographical Dictionary.* Springfield: G. & C. Merriam Co., 1960.
Chongqing: http://www.cqdfz.cn/ (accessed 01/2023).
Croatia: https://dzs.gov.hr (accessed 01/2023).
Estonia: *Statistiche Monatshefte für den Generalbezirk Estland* no. 1–2, 43 (1942). https://www.ra.ee/tuna/en/registration-of-the-population-in-estonia-on-1-december-1941-back-ground-organisation-sources/; https://www.tallinn.ee/en/history-tallinn#:~:text=The%20population%20of%20Tallinn%20decreased,145%20000%20to%20127%20000.
Finland: https://stat.fi/ (accessed 01/2023).
France: http://cassini.ehess.fr/ (accessed 01/2023).
Germany: https://de.wikipedia.org/ (accessed 01/2023).
Great Britain: https://www.ons.gov.uk (accessed 01/2023).
Greece: Biris, Kostas. *Athens from the 19th to the 20th Century.* Athens: Kathydrima Poleodomias kai Istorias ton Athinon, 1966.
Clogg, Richard. *A short history of modern Greece.* Cambridge University Press, 1986.
Darques, Régis. *Salonique au XXe siècle: de la cité ottomane à la métropole grecque.* CNRS, 2000.
Gerontas, D., and D. Skouzes. *The chronicle of watering Athens.* Athens, 1963, 62–63.
Kalantzopoulos, T. *The history of water supply of Athens.* Athens: Palamari Kathrogianni, 1964.
Koliopoulos, Giannēs, John S. Ko-

liopoulos, and Thanos M. Veremis. *Greece: The modern sequel, from 1831 to the present.* NYU Press, 2002.

Hungary: *Budapest szekesfovaros statisztikai évkönyve 1944–1946* [Statistical Yearbook of Budapest, 1944–1946]. Budapest: Budapest Szekesfovaros Statisztikai Hivatala, 1948. Katalin, Csapó and Karner Katalin. *Budapest az egyesítéstől az 1930-as évekig* [Budapest from the unification to the 1930s]. Budapest: Utmutato Kiado, 1999.

Iraq: https://populationstat.com/ (accessed 01/2023).

Israel: https://populationstat.com/ (accessed 01/2023).

Italy: https://www.istat.it (accessed 01/2023).

Japan: Reikichi, Kojima, and Edwin G. Beal. "The Population of the Prefectures and Cities of Japan in Most Recent Times." *The Far Eastern Quarterly* 3, no. 4 (1944), 313–61.

Kuwait: https://populationstat.com/ (accessed 01/2023).

Lebanon: https://populationstat.com/ (accessed 01/2023).

Libya: https://populationstat.com/ (accessed 01/2023).

Myanmar: https://populationstat.com/ (accessed 01/2023).

Netherlands: https://www.cbs.nl/ (accessed 01/2023).

Palestine: https://populationstat.com/ (accessed 01/2023).

Philippines: https://populationstat.com/ (accessed 01/2023).

Poland: https://statlibr.stat.gov.pl/ (accessed 01/2023); Polish academy of sciences committee for demographic studies. *The population of Poland.* Warsaw: Polish Scientific Publishers, 1975.

Russia: http://www.demoscope.ru/ (accessed 01/2023).

Serbia: https://populationstat.com/ (accessed 01/2023).

Spagna: *Ashes and granite: destruction and reconstruction in the Spanish Civil War and its aftermath /.* Muñoz-Rojas, Olivia (2011);

Syria: https://populationstat.com/ (accessed 01/2023).

Ukraine : 2021 Чисельність наявного населення України на 1 січня [2021 Number of Present Population of Ukraine, as of January 1]. Kyiv: State Statistics Service of Ukraine, 2021. https://www.citypopulation.de/ (accessed 01/2023)

Vietnam: https://populationstat.com/ (accessed 01/2023).

Yemen: https://populationstat.com/ (accessed 01/2023).

Romania: Radu, Sageata. "Bucharest. Geographical and geopolitical considerations." *Revista Romana de Geografie Politica* X (2015): 37–56. Populatia republicii populare romane. La 25 ianuarie 1948. Rezultatele provizorii ale recensamantului. https://web.archive.org/web/20200410172753/ https://sas.unibuc.ro/storage/downloads/analize-regionale-9/AG48a.RECENSAMANT48.pdf

• **Violence 2018–2021**
Drawing by Andrea Fantin, Urbicide Task Force.
Source: Armed Conflict Location & Event Data Project (ACLED), https://acleddata.com (10/2022).

• **Disasters 2020–2021**
Drawing by Andrea Fantin, Urbicide Task Force. Source: EM-DAT, CRED / UCLouvain, Brussels, Belgium, www.emdat.be (10/2022) and GRID-Geneva, https://unepgrid.ch/en/about-us/grid (10/2022).

• **Inequality 2009–2019**
Drawing by Andrea Fantin, Urbicide Task Force. Source: local surveys directed by national statistical center of each selected country or reports.
Anguilla: Kairi Consultants Limited in collaboration with the National Assessment Team of Anguilla. *Final report Country Poverty Assessment Anguilla 2007/2009.* Country level, 2010.
Antigua and Barbuda: Sir Arthur Lewis Institute of Social and Economic Studies (SALISES), country level, 2010.
Aruba: Central Bureau of Statistics, country level, 2019.
Bahamas: Bahamas National Statistical Institute, regional level, 2013.
Barbados: Inter-American Development Bank (IDB), country level, 2016.
Belize: Statistical Institute of Belize, country level, 2018.

Bonaire, St. Eusta, Saba: CBS Statistics Netherlands, country level, 2016.

Brazil: IVS Atlas da Vulnerabilidade Social, country level, 2011.

British Virgin Island: Government of the Virgin Islands. *Virgin Islands 2010 Population and Housing Census Report*. Country level, 2010.

Cayman Islands: United Nations Office for the Coordination of Humanitarian Affairs (OCHA), country level, 2022.

Colombia: Departamento Administrativo Nacional de Estadística (DANE), department level, 2016.

Costa Rica: Instituto Nacional de Estadística y Censos (INEC), regional level, 2021.

Dominican Republic: Ministerio de economía, planificación y desarrollo. *Boletín de estadísticas oficiales de pobreza monetaria en república dominicana 2021*. Santo Domingo: Oficinas Gubernamentales, 2021, 9.

Ecuador: Instituto Nacional de Estadistica y Censos (INEC). Compendio de Resultados Encuesta Condiciones de Vida ECV Sexta Ronda 2015. Quito: Instituto Nacional de Estadistica y Censos, 2015.

El Salvador: Dirección General de Estadistica y Censos (DIGESTYC), country level, 2019.

Greanda: Sir Arthur Lewis Institute of Social and Economic Studies (SALISES), country level, 2008.

Guadeloupe: United Nations Office for Disaster Risk Reduction.

Global Assessment Report on Disaster Risk Reduction Guadeloupe. 2015

Guatemala: Istituto Nacional de Estadistica (INE), regional level, 2014.

Guyana: Unidad de Estudios de Políticas Económicas y Sociales del Caribe (UEPESC), country level, 2007.

Haiti: Jadotte, Evans. "Characterization of inequality and poverty in the Republic of Haiti." *Estud soc.* 29 (2022), 7–56.

World Bank, Poverty and Inequality Platform, Gini Index. Washington, DC: World Bank, 2012.

Honduras: Istituto Nacional de Estadistica (INE), regional level, 2018.

Jamaica: Statistical Institute of Jamaica (STATIN), regional level, 2017.

Martinique: Institut National de la statisique et des études économiques (INSEE), country level, 2013.

Mexico: Consejo Nacional de Evaluación de la Política de Desarollo Social (CONEVAL). Indicadores de desigualdad 2010 Oaxaca.

Nicaragua: Istituto Nacional de Estadistica (INE), regional level, 2016.

Panama: Instituto Nacional de Estadística y Censos (INEC), regional level, 2019.

Perù: Instituto Nacional de Estadística e Informatica (INEI), regional level, 2013.

Puerto Rico: US Census Bureau, regional level, 2018.

Saint Kitts and Nevis: Sir Arthur

Lewis Institute of Social and Economic Studies (SALISES), country level, 2011.

Saint Lucia: PovcalNet - World Bank, country level, 2016.

Saint Vincent and the Grenadines: Sir Arthur Lewis Institute of Social and Economic Studies (SALISES), country level, 2008.

Trinidad and Tobago: World Bank, Poverty and Inequality Platform, Gini Index. Washington, DC: World Bank, 1992.

United Stated of America: US Census Bureau, county level, 2020.

Venezuela: Istituto Nacional de Estatistica (INE), regional level, 2013.

2. HISTORICAL EXPERIENCES

• Transformation Map Example [Dresden]

Redrawing by Serena De Conti, Erika Michelazzo, Sarah Mimoun-Rezig, edited by Alessia Cane, Giulia Piacenti, Ambra Tieghi, Urbicide Task Force. Source: Plan von Dresden. Blatt 1 [Altstadt, Neustadt], 1938. Bearb. Vom Vermessungsamt. 1:5000 © Dresden, SLUB, Kartensammlung, SLUB/KS 6048. Google Earth Pro, Image © 2022 GeoBasis_DE/BBKG, image for the year 2008.

• Transformation Map Example [Harare Dzivarasekwa]

Redrawing by Ilaria Casu, Noemi Di Stefano, Laurence Ouellet Quenneville, Alessandra Tore, edited by Alessia Cane, Giulia

Piacenti, Ambra Tieghi, Urbicide Task Force. Source: Google Earth Pro, Image © 2022 Maxar Technologies, image for the year 2008. Google Earth Pro, Image © 2022 Maxar Technologies, image for the year 2021.

• **Transformation Maps Gallery**

Bochum: Redrawing by Erika De Grandis, Valentina Olivieri, Lorenzo Pistore, edited by Alessia Cane, Giulia Piacenti, Ambra Tieghi, Urbicide Task Force.
Bremen: Redrawing by Alessandro Griguol, Nicoló Rigon, Enrico Rocelli, edited by Alessia Cane, Giulia Piacenti, Ambra Tieghi, Urbicide Task Force.
Caen: Redrawing by Denis Caprini, Tommaso Cestaro, Marco Paccagnella, edited by Alessia Cane, Giulia Piacenti, Ambra Tieghi, Urbicide Task Force.
Cape Town: Redrawing by Edna Baroni, Berndette Isermeyer, Marian Lazar, Alice Maset, edited by Alessia Cane, Giulia Piacenti, Ambra Tieghi, Urbicide Task Force.
Corail Cesselesse: Redrawing by Beatrice Cavalcante, Giulia Demontis, Edoardo Lazraj, edited by Alessia Cane, Giulia Piacenti, Ambra Tieghi, Urbicide Task Force.
Coventry: Redrawing by Jacopo Galli, edited by Alessia Cane, Giulia Piacenti, Ambra Tieghi, Urbicide Task Force.
Den Haag: Redrawing by Fulvia Beyer da Silva, Gianluca Driussi,

Lucrezia Pasquali, edited by Alessia Cane, Giulia Piacenti, Ambra Tieghi, Urbicide Task Force.
Detroit: Redrawing by Jacopo Galli, edited by Alessia Cane, Giulia Piacenti, Ambra Tieghi, Urbicide Task Force.
Dresden: Redrawing by Serena De Conti, Erika Michelazzo, Sarah Mimoun-Rezig Sarah, edited by Alessia Cane, Giulia Piacenti, Ambra Tieghi, Urbicide Task Force.
Elbląg: Redrawing by Marco Barberini, Noemi Ena, Lorenzo Lazzarotto, edited by Alessia Cane, Giulia Piacenti, Ambra Tieghi, Urbicide Task Force.
Exeter: Redrawing by Jacopo Galli, edited by Alessia Cane, Giulia Piacenti, Ambra Tieghi, Urbicide Task Force.
Frankfurt am Main: Redrawing by Alberto Allegrini, Alberto Renon, Giovanna Zanotti, edited by Alessia Cane, Giulia Piacenti, Ambra Tieghi, Urbicide Task Force.
Guernica: Redrawing by Chiara Cortivo, Sharon Giammetta, Gianandrea Waldner, edited by Alessia Cane, Giulia Piacenti, Ambra Tieghi, Urbicide Task Force.
Hamburg: Redrawing by Cristina Bicego, Manuel Revoltella, Alessandro Zanin, edited by Alessia Cane, Giulia Piacenti, Ambra Tieghi, Urbicide Task Force.
Harare: Redrawing by Ilaria Casu, Noemi Di Stefano, Laurence Ouellet Quenneville, Alessandra Tore, edited by Alessia Cane, Giulia Piacenti, Ambra Tieghi, Urbicide Task Force.

Ho Chi Minh: Redrawing by Ilaria Signorini, Francesca Dotti, Laura Soardo, edited by Alessia Cane, Giulia Piacenti, Ambra Tieghi, Urbicide Task Force.
Ifo: Redrawing by Davide Bassetto, Elena Cattaruzza, Alice Scopinich, edited by Alessia Cane, Giulia Piacenti, Ambra Tieghi, Urbicide Task Force.
Kaliningrad: Redrawing by Valentin Charles Henri Vianney Bonvarlet, Alice Santi, Alessandro Zanetto, edited by Alessia Cane, Giulia Piacenti, Ambra Tieghi, Urbicide Task Force.
Kassel: Redrawing by Niccolò Andreella, Doina Raluca Iftimie, Viola Volpato, edited by Alessia Cane, Giulia Piacenti, Ambra Tieghi, Urbicide Task Force.
Kuda Ki Basti: Redrawing by Veronica Fornasiero, Anna Gaglione, Silvia Tripodi, edited by Alessia Cane, Giulia Piacenti, Ambra Tieghi, Urbicide Task Force.
Kobane: Redrawing by Jacopo Galli, edited by Alessia Cane, Giulia Piacenti, Ambra Tieghi, Urbicide Task Force.
Kutupalong: Redrawing by Elena Pagliuso, Valentina Santoro, Rebecca Temperanza, edited by Alessia Cane, Giulia Piacenti, Ambra Tieghi.
Lagos: Redrawing by Marco Gentilini, Rachele Lancini, Alice Rampazzo, Asia Trento, edited by Alessia Cane, Giulia Piacenti, Ambra Tieghi, Urbicide Task Force.
Le Havre: Redrawing by Giulia Piacenti, edited by Alessia Cane,

Giulia Piacenti, Ambra Tieghi, Urbicide Task Force.

Lefkõsia/Lefkoşa: Redrawing by Marta Antoniutti, Sara Bertin, Federica Bruni, Mattia Cordioli, Beatrice Didoné, Martina Filippi, Simona Ripepi, Alberta Tiraboschi, Marina Zagato, edited by Alessia Cane, Giulia Piacenti, Ambra Tieghi, Urbicide Task Force.

Lima, Cerro Verde: Redrawing by Nicolò Braga, Massimiliano Coppo, Claudia Monica Lupu, Francisca Pulgar, edited by Alessia Cane, Giulia Piacenti, Ambra Tieghi, Urbicide Task Force.

Lima, Villa El Salvador: Redrawing by Anna Dolcini, Ludovica Farina, Vanessa Finocchiaro, Nazarin Soufian, edited by Alessia Cane, Giulia Piacenti, Ambra Tieghi, Urbicide Task Force.

London: Redrawing by Elena Antonelli, Milo Vianello, edited by Alessia Cane, Giulia Piacenti, Ambra Tieghi, Urbicide Task Force.

Lübeck: Redrawing by Samuel Maso, Virginia Moriconi, Sarnali Razzak, edited by Alessia Cane, Giulia Piacenti, Ambra Tieghi, Urbicide Task Force.

Magdeburg: Redrawing by Chiara Facchin, Sabina Furlan, Sara Menazzi, edited by Alessia Cane, Giulia Piacenti, Ambra Tieghi, Urbicide Task Force.

Marseille: Redrawing by Marco Cau, Luca Forlin, Juliette Selingue, edited by Alessia Cane, Giulia Piacenti, Ambra Tieghi, Urbicide Task Force.

Middelburg: Redrawing by Emma Mattiuzzo, Maria Vittoria Morina, Giovanna Tiso, edited by Alessia Cane, Giulia Piacenti, Ambra Tieghi, Urbicide Task Force.

Milano: Redrawing by Jacopo Galli, edited by Alessia Cane, Giulia Piacenti, Ambra Tieghi, Urbicide Task Force.

(Al) Muharraq: Redrawing by Anna Disarò, Gabriele Feraco, Giulia Loddi, Sara Manente, Emanuele Tonini, edited by Alessia Cane, Giulia Piacenti, Ambra Tieghi, Urbicide Task Force.

München: Redrawing by Mattia Deon, Giovanni Prandstraller, Tommaso Spagnolli, edited by Alessia Cane, Giulia Piacenti, Ambra Tieghi, Urbicide Task Force.

Münster: Redrawing by Jacopo Galli, edited by Alessia Cane, Giulia Piacenti, Ambra Tieghi, Urbicide Task Force.

Nahr el Bared: Redrawing by Jacopo Galli, edited by Alessia Cane, Giulia Piacenti, Ambra Tieghi.

Nairobi: Redrawing by Monica Casolin, Andrea Debiasi, Alberto Farsura, edited by Alessia Cane, Giulia Piacenti, Ambra Tieghi, Urbicide Task Force.

New Orleans: Redrawing by Jacopo Galli, edited by Alessia Cane, Giulia Piacenti, Ambra Tieghi, Urbicide Task Force.

New York: Redrawing by Jacopo Galli, edited by Alessia Cane, Giulia Piacenti, Ambra Tieghi, Urbicide Task Force.

Nürnberg: Redrawing by Alex Dallatorre, Martino Dereani, Veronica Rossa, edited by Alessia Cane, Giulia Piacenti, Ambra Tieghi, Urbicide Task Force.

Orléans: Redrawing by Eduard Adam, Alessandro Barollo, Pietro Cirilli, edited by Alessia Cane, Giulia Piacenti, Ambra Tieghi, Urbicide Task Force.

Pisa: Redrawing by Davide Bergo, Caterina Mattiolo, Livia Sassudelli, edited by Alessia Cane, Giulia Piacenti, Ambra Tieghi, Urbicide Task Force.

Plymouth: Redrawing by Matteo Massolini, Marco Stiz, Gaia Stolzi, edited by Alessia Cane, Giulia Piacenti, Ambra Tieghi, Urbicide Task Force.

Poznań: Redrawing by Federica Borsato, Amina Ettahiry, Beatrice Morsanuto, edited by Alessia Cane, Giulia Piacenti, Ambra Tieghi, Urbicide Task Force.

Rimini: Redrawing by Lucia Andretta, Giulia Cadore, Barbara Pozza, edited by Alessia Cane, Giulia Piacenti, Ambra Tieghi, Urbicide Task Force.

Rotterdam: Redrawing by Gabriele Greco, Maria Benedetta Maioni, Dario Perissinotto, edited by Alessia Cane, Giulia Piacenti, Ambra Tieghi, Urbicide Task Force.

Saint Louis: Redrawing by Jacopo Galli, edited by Alessia Cane, Giulia Piacenti, Ambra Tieghi, Urbicide Task Force.

Saint Malo: Redrawing by Filippo Dal Lago, Marco Dal Lago, Aureliana Rizzo, edited by Alessia Cane, Giulia Piacenti, Ambra Tieghi, Urbicide Task Force.

Terni: Redrawing by Anna Ghillani, Giacomo Niccolò Ghobert, Emiliano Manni, edited by Alessia Cane, Giulia Piacenti, Ambra Tieghi, Urbicide Task Force.
Tindouf: Redrawing by Michela Bitti, Arlette Galdames, Giovanni Papetti, Sara Prinzis, edited by Alessia Cane, Giulia Piacenti, Ambra Tieghi, Urbicide Task Force.
Torino: Redrawing by Martina Bortolotti, Pietro Calusi, Giorgia Pizzanelli, edited by Alessia Cane, Giulia Piacenti, Ambra Tieghi.
Tours: Redrawing by Francesco Deiro, Noemi Montanaro, Francesca Ludovica Reolon, edited by Alessia Cane, Giulia Piacenti, Ambra Tieghi.
Tulsa: Redrawing by Jacopo Galli, edited by Alessia Cane, Giulia Piacenti, Ambra Tieghi.
Valparaiso: Redrawing by Silvia Bidinotto, Giulia Bordignon, Rebecca Traniello Gradassi, edited by Alessia Cane, Giulia Piacenti, Ambra Tieghi.
Venzone: Redrawing by Chiara Semenzin, edited by Alessia Cane, Giulia Piacenti, Ambra Tieghi.
Warsaw: Redrawing by Francesca Angius, Sara Lievi, Ilaria Pani, edited by Alessia Cane, Giulia Piacenti, Ambra Tieghi.
Wien: Redrawing by Alessia Borgato, Sergiu Cristea, Matteo Piva, edited by Alessia Cane, Giulia Piacenti, Ambra Tieghi.
Wroclaw: Redrawing by Elisa Bernard, Elisa Ciuffi, edited by Alessia Cane, Giulia Piacenti, Ambra Tieghi.

Zaatari: Redrawing by Victoria Dolfo, Francesco Londino, Silvia Zannol, Marco Zuanon, edited by Alessia Cane, Giulia Piacenti, Ambra Tieghi, Urbicide Task Force.

• Quantitative and Qualitative Classification
Drawing by Alessia Cane, Giulia Piacenti, Ambra Tieghi, Urbicide Task Force. Source: Bertin, Mattia, Jacopo Galli, and Francesco Rossi. "Retracing reconstruction. An assessment method for urban metamorphoses following extreme events." *Journal of Urban Design* (2022).

³⁻ STRATEGY
• Top Down / Bottom Up
Drawing by Sabrina Righi, Urbicide Task Force. Source: World Bank. *Building for Peace: Reconstruction for Security, Sustainable Peace and Equity in MENA.* Washington, DC: World Bank, 2020.

• Media Attention, Credit & Economic Growth
Drawing by Elisa Vendemini, Urbicide Task Force. Source: Baas, Stephan, Selvaraju Ramasamy, Jenny Dey DePryck and Federica Battista. *Disaster Risk Management System Analyses. A Guide Book.* Roma: FAO, 2008. United Nations and World Bank. *Pathways for Peace: Inclusive Approaches to Preventing Violent Conflict.* Washington, DC: World Bank, 2018.

• Historical Cores and Urban Sprawl
Redrawings by Serena Bolzan, Federica Bresin, Filippo Cracco, Matteo De Bernardini, Giorgia Dal Bianco, Caterina Delaini, Alessandro Dini, Matilde Dufour, Davide Fabrello, Elisa Franceschetti, Nicolò Genovese, Alessia Giampaolino, Filippo Giancola, Francesco Martini, Sabrina Righi, Andrea Russo, Marco Santoni, Akira Sato, Maria Concetta Savignano, Giulia Simonetto, Giorgia Soini, Giorgio Trivellin, Marco Turcato, Stefano Zugno, edited by Elisa Vendemini, Urbicide Task Force.

• Historical Cores and Urban Sprawl Under Pressure
Aleppo redrawing by Dante Bisutti, Margherita Cisamolo, Carolina Coltelli, Gianmarco Ippino, Silvia Marchetti, Annalisa Moser, Ilaria Pezzini, Giulia Piacenti, Elisa Vendemini, Rossella Villani.
Mariupol redrawing by Serena Pappalardo, Elisa Vendemini, Urbicide Task Force. Source: UADamage. Updated 10/2022.
Valparaiso redrawing by Serena Pappalardo, Elisa Vendemini, Urbicide Task Force. Source: SECPLA, Municipalidad Valparaíso, 2014.

• From Sprawl to Cells
Mosul destruction redrawing by Serena Bolzan, Federica Bresin, Filippo Cracco, Matteo De Bernardini, Giorgia Dal Bianco, Caterina Delaini, Alessandro Dini,

Matilde Dufour, Davide Fabrello, Elisa Franceschetti, Nicolò Genovese, Alessia Giampaolino, Filippo Giancola, Francesco Martini, Sabrina Righi, Andrea Russo, Marco Santoni, Akira Sato, Maria Concetta Savignano, Giulia Simonetto, Giorgia Soini, Giorgio Trivellin, Marco Turcato, Stefano Zugno, edited by Serena Pappalardo, Urbicide Task Force. Mosul cells process and final urban form by Serena Pappalardo, Urbicide Task Force.

• **Advantages**
Drawing by Sabrina Righi, Urbicide Task Force. Source: World Bank. *Building for Peace: Reconstruction for Security, Sustainable Peace and Equity in MENA*. Washington, DC: World Bank, 2020.

• **Phases of Emergency**
Drawing by Elisa Vendemini, Urbicide Task Force. Source: Federal Emergency Management Agency (FEMA). *Four Phases of Emergency Management*. Washington, DC: FEMA, 2020.

4- SUSTAINABLE TRANSITION
• **Features of the Historical Core**
Drawing by Ambra Tieghi, Urbicide Task Force. Source: Alberto Bertollo, Greta Cattelan, Rosa Da Boit, Simone Dalla Rosa, Piera Favaretto, Roberto Ferraresi, Marco Marino, Alessandro Rossi, Giacomo Savegnago, Carolina Scorsone, Chiara Semenzin, Debora Tarzia. *Restauro Urbano*

Sostenibile: Nuove Strategie per i Centri Storici. MA theses, Università Iuav di Venezia, 2017.

• **Filling the Technological Gap: The Leap Forward**
Drawing by Sabrina Righi, Urbicide Task Force. Source: Ragette, Friedrich. *Traditional Domestic Architecture of the Arab Region*. Fellbach Vereinigte Arabische Emirate: Edition Axel Menges American University of Sharjah, 2003, 252.

• **Models of Decentralized Administration**
Drawing by Chiara Semenzin, Urbicide Task Force. Source: Frey, Bruno, and Reiner Eichenberger. *The New Democratic Federalism of Europe: Functional, Overlapping and Competing Jurisdiction*. Cheltenham: Edward Elgar, 1999.

• **Circular Scenarios**
Drawing by Sabrina Righi, Urbicide Task Force. Based on a design by Urbicide Task Force, consultants Enrico Guastaroba, Luca Panzeri.

6- DESIGN
• **Urban Restoration Tools**
Drawing by Chiara Semenzin, Urbicide Task Force. Source: Leonardo Benevolo, Pier Luigi Cervellati, Italo Insolera con Ufficio Centro Storico della Ripartizione Urbanistica del Comune di Palermo. *Piano Particolareggiato Esecutivo Centro Storico*. Comune di Paler-

mo, Assessorato all'Urbanistica e centro storico, 1989.

• **Urban Restoration Table**
Drawing by Ambra Tieghi, Alessia Cane, Urbicide Task Force. Source: Giulia Piacenti. *Sustainable Reconstruction for Aleppo*. MA thesis, Università Iuav di Venezia, 2016.

• **Urban Triggers: Backbones**
Drawings by Ambra Tieghi and Alessia Cane, Urbicide Task Force. Sources: Giulia Piacenti. *Sustainable Reconstruction for Aleppo: Historical core*. MA thesis, Università Iuav di Venezia, 2016; Maria Giulia Pistonese. *Urbicide Rural Syria: Reconstruction of villages: Adnaniyeh*. MA thesis, Università Iuav di Venezia, 2018; Leonardo Brancaleoni. *Urbicide Rural Syria: Reconstruction of villages: Sheran*. MA thesis, Università Iuav di Venezia, 2018; Matteo Bertazzon, Davide Bertin and Simone Giacchetto. *Charbagh City: Towards a Sustainable City*. MA thesis, Università Iuav di Venezia, 2019; Matilde Dufour and Alessia Giampaolino. *Urbicide Mosul: Triggers for reconstruction: Productive orography*. MA thesis, Università Iuav di Venezia, 2019; Matteo De Bernardini, Elisa Franceschetti and Maria Concetta Savignano. *Urbicide Mosul: Triggers for reconstruction: Informal structure*. MA thesis, Università Iuav di Venezia, 2019.

- **Urban Triggers:**
Induced Design
Drawings by Ambra Tieghi, Urbicide Task Force. Sources: Maddalena Meneghello, Antonio Signori and Sonia Zucchelli. *Urbicide Rural Syria: Reconstruction of villages: Al Jobeh – Jrajeer.* MA thesis, Università Iuav di Venezia, 2018; Filippo Cracco and Filippo Giancola. *Urbicide Mosul: Triggers for reconstruction: Borders Redefinition.* MA thesis, Università Iuav di Venezia, 2019; Dario Perissinotto. *Ukraine Reconstruction: The case of Irpin.* MA thesis, Università Iuav di Venezia, 2023

- **Patterns of Growing**
Evolutionary Mechanisms
Drawing by Sabrina Righi, Elisa Vendemini, Urbicide Task Force. Source: mathematical elaborations on the urban pattern of Tripoli, Cairo, Hamburg, Lübeck, Tripoli carried out by *Francesco Rossi*, Department of Mathematics "Tullio Levi-Civita," Università di Padova.

THANKS TO:
Graduate Students 2016
– Sustainable Reconstruction for Aleppo: Dante Bisutti, Margherita Cisamolo, Carolina Coltelli, Gianmarco Ippino, Silvia Marchetti, Annalisa Moser, Ilaria Pezzini, Giulia Piacenti, Elisa Vendemini, Rossella Villani.

Graduate Students 2017
– Sustainable Urban Restoration: New Strategies for Historical Cores: Alberto Bertollo, Greta Cattelan, Simone Della Rosa, Rosa Da Boit, Piera Favaretto, Roberto Ferraresi, Marco Marino, Alessandro Rossi, Carolina Scorsone, Chiara Semenzin, Debora Tarzia.

Graduate Students 2018
– Urbicide Rural Syria: Reconstruction of Villages: Lorenzo Abate, Stefano Bortolato, Leonardo Brancaleoni, Michele Brusutti, Stefano Busetto, Pietropaolo Cristini, Susanna De Vido, Martina Fadanelli, Martina Germanà, Maria Guerra, Irene Guizzo, Michele Maniero, Maddalena Meneghello, Silvia Pellizzon, Camilla Pettinelli, Mariagiulia Pistonese, Giacomo Raffaelli, Elena Salvadore, Antonio Signori, Sonia Zucchelli.

Graduate Students 2019
– Urbicide Mosul: Triggers for Reconstruction: Serena Bolzan, Federica Bresin, Filippo Cracco, Matteo De Bernardini, Giorgia Dal Bianco, Caterina Delaini, Alessandro Dini, Matilde Dufour, Davide Fabrello, Elisa Franceschetti, Nicolò Genovese, Alessia Giampaolino, Filippo Giancola, Francesco Martini, Sabrina Righi, Andrea Russo, Marco Santoni, Akira Sato, Maria Concetta Savignano, Giulia Simonetto, Giorgia Soini, Giorgio Trivellin, Marco Turcato, Stefano Zugno.

Graduate Students 2020
– Urbicide Afghanistan: Matteo Bertazzon, Davide Bertin, Beatrice Bertoluzzo, Angela D'Alessio, Camilla Donadon, Simone Giacchetto, Vittoria Ianigro, Filippo Lazzer, Ibrahim Mansi, Alessandro Mazzi, Giorgio Pasqualetto, Giulia Alessandra Pozzan, Greta Sadushi, Chiara Sanguin.

Graduate Students 2021
– Architecture in Conflict: Cyprus & Bahrein: Marta Antoniutti, Sara Bertin, Federica Bruni, Mattia Cordioli, Beatrice Didonè, Anna Disarò, Gabriele Feraco, Martina Filippi, Giulia Loddi, Sara Manente, Beatrice Pelizzo, Angela Pranovi, Simona Ripepi, Alberta Tiraboschi, Emanuele Tonini, Marina Zagato.

Graduate Students 2022
– The Mediterranean System: Althea Andreoni, Davide Bergo, Piero Bigatello, Alessia Cane, Matteo Ergazzori, Katjia Kovačič, Manuel Longa, Isabella Lovato, Emma Madinelli, Caterina Mattiolo, Aureliana Rizzo, Francesco Tassello, Ambra Tieghi, Vittoria Vesentini, Viola Volpato.

Graduate Students 2023
Fulvia Beyer da Silva, Francesca Caloi, Dario Perissinotto, Melissa Rossetti.

CREDITS

This book was made possible thanks to the support of Nohad Haj Salih – I.Barbon Shipping and Logistics